The CKFM Bonnie Stern Cookbook

THE CKFM

BONNIE STERN COOKBOOK

*A fundraising project
in support of the Hospital for Sick Children*

A RANDOM HOUSE/SOMERVILLE HOUSE BOOK
TORONTO

Copyright © 1987 by Bonnie Stern
All rights reserved under International and
Pan-American Copyright Conventions.

Published in Canada by
Random House of Canada Limited, Toronto

CANADIAN CATALOGUING IN PUBLICATION DATA
Stern, Bonnie
    The Bonnie Stern cookbook
Includes index.
ISBN 0-394-22022-1
1. Cookery.   I. Title.
TX715.S74   1987   641.5   C86-094498-0

Design: C.P. Wilson Graphic Communication
Cover photographs: Ruth Kaplan
Illustrations: Bo-Kim Louie and David Mazierski
Editorial: Shelley Tanaka

Produced by
Somerville House Books Ltd.
24 Dinnick Crescent
Toronto, Ontario M4N 1L5

Printed and bound in Canada

DEDICATION

For my special children: Mark, who eats nothing at all; Anna, who eats everything in sight; and Fara, who helps me cook. And for all the other special children including:

Anne, Bryn, Claire and Jessica Abraham; Daniel, Jeremy and Mikhel Adiram; Miriam and Gillian Aiken; David and Lisa Agar; Alexandra and Brooks Allen; Rena Andoh; Annabel and Guy Aspler; Joshua Belvedere; Jordan and Dara Benson; Emily Berg; Amy Boniuk; Jonathan Brown; Mara and Naomi Brown; Lauren Bulwa; Alison Carr; Jordan and Julian Caspari; Brian Costello Jr.; Erin and Ryan Day; Andrew, Owen and Shawn Duckman; Aaron, Dina and Jonathan Egier; John-Michael Erlendson; Amber and Dana Evans; Benji Feferman; Elizabeth Feld; Elyssa Forman; Robin, Ryan and Sharon Franklin; Laura and Adam Garetson; Amber, Robin and Rory Ginsberg; Aubrey, Shannon, Stacie and Trevor Glazman; Jonathon and Sarah Gleeson; Alanna and Simon Golden; Cristine and Paul Gould; Eryn and Jared Green; Martha and Trevor Haldenby; Debra and Naomi Hamer; Lisa and Paul Hoffman; Bryan Holt; Leanne and Michelle Iceruk; Alexandre, Michelle, Nicole and Stephanie Karkic; Blagoja Karkic; Jason, Mark and Marni Kimmelman; Emily and Matthew Kindred; Christina and John Klich; Joshua and Zackary Kline; Michael Konviser; Bess Kosinec; Charles and Meredith Krangle; Cheryl Krangle; Elana, Joshua and Sherri Lavine; Karen, Leslie and Robyn Lerer; Liana and Maddi Levinson; Brian and Rhonda Lewis; Philip and Sarah Lewis; Jeff, John and Susie Lindsay; Mia, Rachel and Sherri Linzon; Ben and Kate Lollar; Brian, Kerry and Kevin Lollar; Emily, Nathan and Tabitha Lollar; André Marie; Christine and Laura Masching; Jeremy and Shawn Melamed; Erin, Kelley and Meredith Melnyck; Courtney and Kimberly Moore; Adam and Daniel Nathanson; Marshall and Matthew Newton; Conan and Meaghan O'Brien; Caleigh and Jamie Pacini; Lisa Porter; Jordan and Steven Prussky; Anthony, Lorne and Randi Rose; Alana and Ashley Salzberg; Bethany, Lyndsay, Megan and Natasha Saunders; Abigail and Rachel Shime; Andrea and Julia Smith; Alison Soles; Jonathon, Jordan and Justin Soles; Marshall Starkman; David and Randi Swimmer; Michael Tile; Daniel and Michael Tward; Douglas and Michael Weil; Michael Werry; Jason and Jenny White; Avi and Laurie Wolfand; Jason Wright; Christopher Yancey; Carly and Jarett Zaidlin; Kevin and Shauna Zeileg; Sasha Zeileg; Alison, Jason and Sean Zweig; Allison and Robbie Zweig, and many more.

Preface	8
Appetizers	10
Soups	26
Main Courses	41
Pastas and Light Meals	69
Vegetables	86
Salads and Salad Dressings	99
Breads and Muffins	112
Cakes	125
Cookies and Chocolates	136
Desserts and Pastries	145
Especially for Kids	164
Index	184
A Note on Metric	192

Preface

Talking about food on the radio is a challenge. You can't see the food, and you can't smell it. So when listeners tell me that they were so excited after hearing a recipe that they just had to cook it right away, or when they say they almost had an accident trying to copy down the recipe in their cars with lipstick on a Kleenex, I feel wonderful knowing that I am reaching people and conveying my enthusiasm for food.

I remember the first recipe I "cooked" on "Hour Toronto Magazine" eight years ago. I made the shortbread cookies on page 137. Peter Pacini, our producer, had taken one of my cooking classes and asked me to do something special for Christmas. I don't know if he asked me back because of listener response or because the cookies I brought in were so delicious, but I was delighted. And it has been a wonderful relationship ever since.

Another recipe that I remember well was the one for rice pudding on page 151. Who would have thought that so many people were looking for the great rice pudding recipe of all time? That was the recipe that broke the bank, so to speak. Until then listeners could call in for a recipe, but after 450 people phoned in twelve hours, we had to change the policy. Now if you want a copy of a recipe, you have to send a stamped self-addressed envelope!

It's a pleasure doing the shows with Judy Webb. She is entertaining, clever, and seems to know just the right amount about cooking to ask the right questions. Sometimes when I go on and on, blithely assuming that everyone knows what I'm talking about, she gently brings me back to earth and has me go over the instructions that everyone really needs to know. This is especially true when I'm explaining how to make pastry. But Judy can't complain about her problems with pastry anymore. Check the photos on the back of this book for proof that she has finally received her promised pastry lesson from me. She did a great job, and I was very proud of her!

A special thank-you goes to Lynn Pickering, the associate producer of "Hour Toronto Magazine". Not only was this cookbook her idea and pet project, but Lynn is the person who keeps everything organized from day to day. She books my spots, sends out the recipes, keeps track of everything and makes sure that when people write in and say, "I'm going to New York in two days and I need Bonnie's list of places to eat right away," it always gets there on time. I'm indebted to Lynn and Renate Brickman for retyping this entire manuscript after I updated all the recipes, which saved me hours of work. But most of all I want to thank Lynn for giving me the chance to make a significant contribution to the Hospital for Sick Children through this book. Since I've had Mark and Anna, a whole new world has opened up to me (not to mention the new experience of trying to get children to eat!). I'm grateful to have this opportunity to do something for all children, especially those who do not have all the love and good health they deserve.

Many people have made it possible for the Children's Fund to receive the maximum amount of money through the sale of this book. Special thanks go to Jane Somerville, Shelley Tanaka, Bo-Kim Louie, Ruth Kaplan, Catherine Wilson and especially to Ed Carson, Random House of Canada.

And finally I want to thank all those who listen to the "Hour Toronto Magazine" show. When you write in and say you love the show and want a recipe, it makes my day! And to everyone who listens to the show, I want to apologize for talking so fast all the time, but as you probably know by now, it's hard for me to stay calm and speak slowly when I'm talking about food—I love it too much and have so much to say! So this book is really dedicated to you.

Bonnie Stern
Toronto, 1987

Appetizers

Olive Mustard Spread

Makes 1½ cups/375 mL

Pauline Wayne is the inventor and manufacturer of two great Canadian mustards —Honeycup Mustard and The Original Canadian Beer Mustard. This is a wonderful spread for French bread or crackers and can also be used as a sauce for cold cuts. Although it can be used directly from the refrigerator, it is creamier at room temperature.

Although the Kalamata olives must be pitted, I think their flavour is far superior to most canned, pitted olives. Pit the olives with a cherry pitter—it works!

8 oz	black olives (preferably Kalamata), pitted	250 g
2 tbsp	Original Canadian Beer Mustard (or other coarse-grained mustard)	25 mL
½	small red onion, diced	½
2 tbsp	chopped fresh basil or parsley	25 mL
½ tsp	freshly ground pepper	2 mL
½ cup	unsalted butter, at room temperature	125 mL

1 Place the pitted olives in food processor or blender and process until finely chopped.

2 Add the remaining ingredients and process until smooth.

3 Taste and adjust seasoning as necessary.

Smoked Salmon Canapés

Makes about 2 cups/500 mL

This recipe is a great way to use up little bits of leftover smoked salmon. Serve it for snacks, as an appetizer, or in sandwiches for lunch.

8 oz	smoked salmon	250 g
½ cup	unsalted butter	125 mL
½ cup	Ricotta cheese, well drained	125 mL
2 tbsp	lemon juice	25 mL
	Pumpernickel	
	Sprigs fresh dill	
1 oz	salmon caviar (optional)	30 g
	Lemon slices	

1. Chop the smoked salmon in a food processor or mince finely with a knife.
2. Combine the salmon and butter until smooth. Blend in the Ricotta cheese and lemon juice. (Add pepper if you wish.)
3. Cut the pumpernickel into 1½-in/4-cm squares or rounds and pipe or spoon the salmon mixture on them.
4. Decorate with a sprig of dill or a few drops of salmon caviar.
5. Place on a serving platter and garnish with lemon slices.

Smoked Salmon Pâté

Makes 1 loaf

This is my version of one of Toronto's most popular take-out pâtés. It really is spectacular.

When you serve anything made with smoked salmon to guests, they feel special. Smoked salmon is rich, elegant and luxurious in texture, with a price to match. When you use it in this recipe, however, a small amount of salmon serves a lot of people, and your guests will still feel special.

This recipe will serve 12 to 16 people, but it can also be halved.

1	**envelope unflavoured gelatine**	1
¼ cup	**cold water**	50 mL
1 cup	**whipping cream**	250 mL
12 oz	**smoked salmon, diced**	375 g
4 oz	**cream cheese**	125 g
1 cup	**sour cream (preferably Astro)**	250 mL
2 tbsp	**lemon juice**	25 mL
	Salt and freshly ground pepper to taste	
10 oz	**spinach, cooked and squeezed dry**	300 g
4	**vine leaves, rinsed and patted dry**	4

1. Sprinkle the gelatine over the cold water in a small saucepan. Allow it to rest for 5 minutes. Heat gently and stir to dissolve the gelatine.
2. Whip the cream lightly until soft peaks form.
3. Place the smoked salmon in a food processor fitted with the steel knife (this can also be done in a blender). Chop the smoked salmon coarsely.
4. Add the cream cheese and blend until the cream cheese is smooth. Add the sour cream and blend well. Blend in the lemon juice, salt and pepper (the amount of salt you add will depend on the saltiness of the salmon).
5. Add the gelatine to the mixture in the food processor or blender and combine well.
6. Add all but a few spoonfuls of the mixture to the whipped cream and fold in gently but thoroughly. Taste and adjust the seasoning.
7. Add the spinach to the remaining salmon mixture in the food processor or blender and blend well. Taste and adjust the seasoning.
8. Line an 8-inch x 4-inch/1.5-L loaf pan with plastic wrap and line with the vine leaves. Add half the salmon mixture and spread out evenly. Spread all of the spinach mixture over that. Top with remaining salmon mixture.
9. Cover with plastic wrap and refrigerate for at least 3 hours. Unmould onto a pretty loaf plate and decorate with lemon slices, tomato roses (see page 20), smoked salmon roses and/or watercress.

Crêpes with Smoked Salmon and Cream Cheese

Serves 6 (makes 12 crêpes)

This is a very elegant appetizer. If you have difficulty making crêpes in a traditional omelette or crêpe pan, use a non-stick pan or a specially designed "upside-down" crêpe pan.

CRÊPES	4	eggs	4
	1 cup	all-purpose flour	250 mL
	½ tsp	salt	2 mL
	1 tbsp	sugar	15 mL
	1 cup	milk	250 mL
	¼ cup	water	50 mL
	2 tbsp	unsalted butter, melted	25 mL
FILLING	12 oz	cream cheese	375 g
	¼ cup	lemon juice	50 mL
	¼ cup	finely chopped fresh dill	50 mL
		Salt and freshly ground pepper to taste	
	1 lb	smoked salmon, thinly sliced	500 g

1. Prepare the crêpe batter by combining all the crêpe ingredients. Let rest, covered, for 1 hour.

2. Heat an 8-in/20-cm crêpe or omelette pan with 1 tbsp/15 mL additional unsalted butter (unsalted butter burns and sticks less easily than salted butter). Make the crêpes by adding a ladleful of batter. Swirl it in the pan and pour the excess batter back into the batter bowl. Cook the crêpe until brown, then flip. Cook the second side. Repeat with the remaining batter (you should have about 12 crêpes).

3. To make the filling, combine the cheese, lemon juice and dill. Add salt and pepper to taste. Spread filling on each crêpe and arrange two slices of salmon on each. Fold each crêpe in half and then in quarters (see illustration).

4. Serve two crêpes per person as an appetizer, or serve like party sandwiches for hors d'oeuvres.

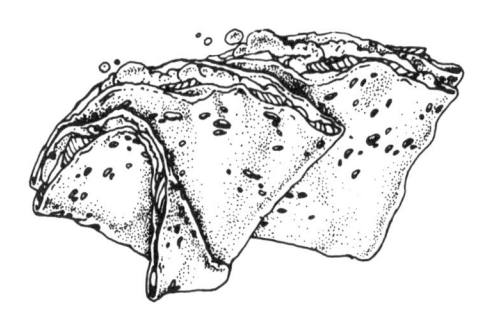

Muffalata Olive Salad

Makes approx. 3 cups/750 mL

This popular New Orleans olive salad is the base for the city's most famous sandwich. The sandwich is made with a large, flat sesame bun, lots of sliced meats and cheeses and then topped with this salad.

You can use this as part of an antipasto platter, serve it as a "spread" with ham or salami sandwiches, or toss it with 1½ lb/750 g cooked pasta and serve it hot or cold. Or toss with 2 lb/1 kg cooked red potatoes for a wonderful potato salad.

2 cups	green olives stuffed with pimentos	500 mL
½ cup	black olives (preferably Kalamata), pitted	125 mL
1	4-oz/125-g jar marinated artichokes	1
2 tbsp	diced pimento	25 mL
1 tbsp	hot pickled peppers, finely chopped	15 mL
2 tbsp	pickled pepper juice	25 mL
½ tsp	oregano	2 mL
½ tsp	freshly ground pepper	2 mL
2	cloves garlic, minced	2
2	anchovy fillets, minced	2
2 tbsp	capers	25 mL
½ cup	extra-virgin olive oil	125 mL

1 Smash the olives and chop them coarsely. Chop the artichokes and combine with the olives (use the juices of the artichokes as well).

2 Add all the remaining ingredients and combine well. Taste and adjust seasonings if necessary. (The texture of the mixture should be semi-pureed.)

Hundred Corner Shrimp Balls

Makes approx. 36 balls

These little dim sum treats are so delicious and very easy to prepare. They are great hot or at room temperature and can be served with a dipping sauce of hot chili sauce or salt seasoned with a little curry powder, five spice powder or crushed Szechuan peppercorns. They can be made ahead and reheated in the oven.

Any white-fleshed fish fillets can be used instead of the shrimp. The shrimp paste itself (without the bread cubes) can also be poached in water and served as dumplings in soup, or can be pan fried as little shrimp patties.

12	slices white bread	12
1 lb	raw shrimp, shelled and cleaned	500 g
1	egg white	1
1 tbsp	rice wine	15 mL
1 tsp	salt	5 mL
1 tsp	minced ginger root	5 mL
1 tbsp	minced green onion	15 mL
¼ cup	minced water chestnuts	50 mL
2 tbsp	cornstarch	25 mL
4 cups	peanut oil for deep-frying	1 L

1. Remove the crusts from the bread. Dice the bread into ¼-in/5-mm cubes. Place on a cookie sheet and dry out in a very low oven (200°F/90°C).

2. Pat the shrimp dry and mince in a food processor or blender. Blend in all the remaining ingredients except the oil.

3. With wet hands, shape the shrimp paste into 1-in/2.5-cm balls and roll in the bread cubes. Press the cubes firmly into the shrimp mixture.

4. Heat the oil in a wok or deep, wide pot to 375°F/190°C. Cook the shrimp balls in batches until nicely browned and cooked through (this should only take 4 to 5 minutes). Drain on paper towels.

Chèvre Spread

Makes approx. 2 cups/500 mL

This flavourful, tangy spread is great served with bread or crackers. It can also be piped into mushroom caps, cherry tomatoes, cucumber slices, or into Belgian endive leaves. Buy soft, unripened goat cheese for this recipe, preferably without a rind.

12 oz	unripened chèvre (remove rind if any)	375 g
½ cup	unsalted butter	125 mL
1	small clove garlic, minced	1
½ tsp	Tabasco sauce	2 mL
¼ tsp	thyme	1 mL
¼ tsp	rosemary	1 mL
¼ tsp	freshly ground pepper	1 mL
2 tbsp	finely chopped black olives	25 mL
2 tbsp	finely chopped sun-dried tomatoes	25 mL

1. Cream the chèvre with the butter until smooth.
2. Blend in the garlic, Tabasco, thyme, rosemary and pepper.
3. Stir in the olives and tomatoes. (Do not blend because you want them to remain as little colourful pieces suspended in the mixture.)

Cajun Spiced Almonds

Makes approx. 3 cups/750 mL

These spicy almonds are a wonderful way to wake up your appetite before dinner or are delicious as a snack any time. Don't serve too many, though, as it is very hard to stop eating them! The idea to glaze the nuts with corn syrup came from Abby Mandel, who is well known throughout North America for her food processor recipes. The nuts are not sweet, but glazed beautifully.

These can also be frozen. If they are not crisp enough, rebake for 15 minutes before serving.

2 tbsp	unsalted butter	25 mL
¼ cup	corn syrup	50 mL
2 tbsp	water	25 mL
1½ tsp	salt	7 mL
1 tsp	cayenne pepper	5 mL
2 tsp	paprika	10 mL
2 tsp	Tabasco sauce	10 mL
1 tsp	freshly ground white pepper	5 mL
1 lb	whole almonds with skins	500 g

1 Preheat the oven to 250°F/120°C. Line a cookie sheet with aluminum foil or parchment paper.

2 Place the butter, corn syrup, water, salt, cayenne, paprika, Tabasco and white pepper in a heavy saucepan. Bring to a boil.

3 Stir in the almonds and coat them well.

4 Spread the almonds on the cookie sheet and bake for 1 hour. Stir every 15 minutes to separate the nuts.

APPETIZERS

Grilled Carpaccio Salad

Serves 8

Carpaccio is an Italian specialty where the meat is usually served raw. In this version, the meat is coated with a mustard glaze and cooked briefly but served very rare. If you prefer meat more well done, cook it a little longer.
This can be served as an appetizer or for a special lunch.

ROAST	2 lb	filet roast, trimmed*	1 kg
	3 tbsp	Dijon mustard	50 mL
	1 tsp	Worcestershire sauce	5 mL
	1 tsp	soy sauce	5 mL
SALAD	8	large leaves ruby lettuce or radicchio	8
	4 oz	fresh mushrooms, thinly sliced	125 g
	4 oz	Parmigiano Reggiano, thinly sliced**	125 g
	2 tbsp	lemon juice	25 mL
	½ cup	extra-virgin olive oil	125 mL
	½ tsp	salt	2 mL
	¼ tsp	freshly ground pepper	1 mL
SAUCE	1 cup	fresh basil or parsley leaves	250 mL
	1	slice white bread	1
	2	anchovy fillets	2
	2 tbsp	red wine vinegar	25 mL
	⅓ cup	extra-virgin olive oil	75 mL
	¼ tsp	freshly ground pepper	1 mL

1. Preheat the oven to 450°F/225°C. Pat the filet dry.
2. Combine the mustard with the Worcestershire and soy sauce. Spread this mixture over the filet. Place the filet on a roasting rack and roast for 10 minutes. Remove from the oven and cool. (The roast will be very rare.) Freeze for 40 minutes for easier slicing.
3. With a very sharp carving knife, slice the filet very very thin.
4. On each serving plate arrange a leaf of lettuce. Arrange a few slices of the filet on top. Decorate with the mushrooms and thin slices of cheese, but allow some of the filet to show through.
5. Combine the lemon juice, ½ cup/125 mL olive oil, salt and pepper and drizzle over the salads.
6. Combine all the sauce ingredients in a food processor or blender. Place a spoonful on each serving.

* *This is probably a little more filet than you will need for eight servings. However, if you use less, it will be almost impossible to slice it all very thin. Use up any extra in salads or sandwiches.*

** *Parmigiano Reggiano is a crumbly cheese, so do not be surprised if it breaks into small pieces when you try to slice it. Just use the thinnest best slices in the salad and save any thicker pieces for another use.*

Olivada and Mascarpone Torta

Makes 3 cups/750 mL

This layered cheese spread is a spectacular company treat. Any leftovers can easily be made into sandwiches. I have even tossed this mixture with cooked fettuccine, a little butter and Parmesan cheese for a sensational pasta dish.

Mascarpone is a creamy Italian cheese that is becoming more and more available in North America. It is also being produced in Canada now; the domestic variety would work well in this recipe and cost considerably less than the imported product. If you cannot find Mascarpone, use 1 lb/500 g cream cheese beaten with 1 cup/ 250 mL unsalted butter as a substitute.

Another great version of this can be made using a half recipe of pesto sauce (see page 73) instead of the olivada.

	1	clove garlic, minced	1
	½	red onion, minced	½
	3 tbsp	minced fresh parsley or basil	50 mL
	8 oz	black olives (preferably Kalamata), pitted and coarsely chopped	250 g
	½ tsp	freshly ground pepper	2 mL
	½ cup	unsalted butter, at room temperature	125 mL
	1½ lb	Mascarpone cheese	750 g
GARNISH		Fresh sprigs basil	
		Tomato roses	

1. To make the olivada, combine the garlic, onion, parsley, olives, pepper and butter in a food processor or blender. Blend until you have a paste-like mixture.
2. Line a 4-cup/1-L soufflé dish or mould with plastic wrap.
3. Beat the cheese until smooth.
4. Spread one-quarter of the Mascarpone in the bottom of the mould. Top with one-third of the olivada. Continue layering until the cheese and olive mixture are used up, ending with a cheese layer.
5. Wrap well in plastic wrap and refrigerate for a few hours or overnight.
6. To serve, unwrap and unmould on a serving plate and serve with crackers and/or French bread. Garnish the top with fresh basil leaves and place a few tomato roses around the sides (see illustrations).

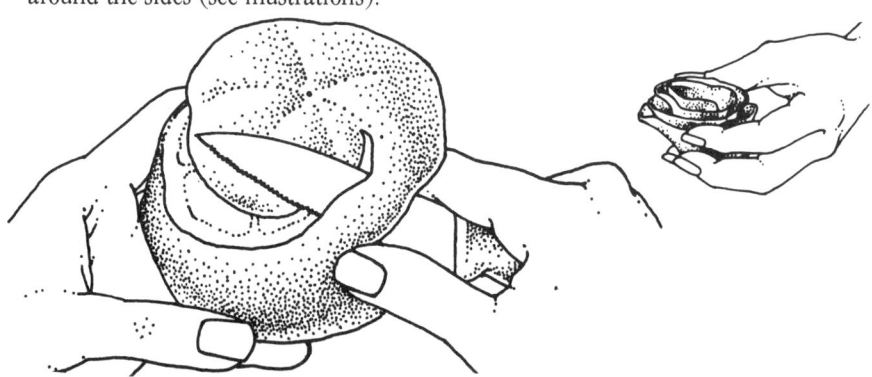

Smoked Trout Tartare

Makes approx. 60 hors d'oeuvres

Every year when Jacques Pépin comes to my school to teach, he causes a sensation. Not only does he teach delicious recipes and excellent cooking techniques, he is also perfectly charming—students fall in love with him immediately. When he leaves, everyone, including the worn-out staff, rush home to prepare his recipes.

This recipe is based on one of his dishes. He used fresh raw salmon, but I like to use smoked salmon or smoked trout instead. That way, even fussy eaters will love it.

You can use this as a spread with black bread, crackers or buttered toast, or serve it in Belgian endive leaves or hollowed-out cucumber slices.

4	smoked trout (about 8 oz/250 g each)	4
¼ cup	extra-virgin olive oil	50 mL
⅓ cup	lemon juice	75 mL
½ tsp	grated lemon peel	2 mL
¼ cup	chopped fresh chives or green onions	50 mL
¼ cup	chopped fresh parsley	50 mL
¼ cup	chopped fresh dill or basil	50 mL
½ tsp	Tabasco sauce	2 mL
2 tbsp	capers	25 mL
½ tsp	freshly ground pepper	2 mL

1. Remove the skin from the trout. Remove the meat from the bones and flake it into a bowl. (The fish can be flaked or you can chop it a little finer with a knife or in the food processor. But do not puree it.) You should have approximately 1 lb/500 g.

2. Combine the remaining ingredients and toss with the trout until very well combined. Taste and adjust the seasonings if necessary.

Scallops Provençal

Serves 6 to 8

Scallops are my very favourite seafood. They are sweet, succulent and tender. I love both their taste and texture. This recipe is based on one I tasted in Paris and whenever I make it, I think of all the delicious places I visit when I'm there.

I always buy fresh scallops because their texture is usually far superior to the frozen. And for this recipe I like to use the larger sea scallops rather than the very small bay ones.

This can be served with lots of French bread or it can be combined with fettuccine for a wonderful pasta dish. Use 1 lb/500 g fettuccine.

¾ cup	unsalted butter	175 mL
3	cloves garlic, finely chopped	3
1	shallot, finely chopped	1
3	tomatoes, peeled, seeded and finely chopped	3
⅓ cup	dry white wine	75 mL
1½ lb	scallops	750 g
¼ cup	chopped fresh parsley	50 mL
	Salt and freshly ground pepper to taste	

1. Melt one-third of the butter in a large skillet and add the garlic and shallots. Cook until very fragrant and tender, but do not brown.

2. Add the tomatoes and wine and cook until the sauce is reduced and somewhat thicker, about 5 minutes.

3. In another skillet, melt one-third of the butter and add the scallops. Cover loosely with buttered parchment or waxed paper and cook for 3 to 4 minutes or until they are just barely cooked. Add half the parsley, taste and season with lots of freshly ground pepper and salt.

4. Add the scallops and any juices to the tomato mixture. Stir in the remaining butter and allow to melt.

5. Serve the scallops with the remaining parsley sprinkled on top. Serve with French bread.

Szechuan Orange Chicken Wings

Makes approx. 24 pieces

This is a great recipe for those who love Szechuan orange chicken. It is easier than the stir-fried version done with the chicken meat. You can serve it with rice for a main course, but I like to serve it as finger food as an appetizer.

	2 lb	chicken wings	1 kg
MARINADE	3	cloves garlic, minced	3
	4 tsp	minced ginger root	20 mL
	3	green onions, minced	3
	⅓ cup	Hoisin sauce	75 mL
	1 tbsp	hot Chinese chili paste	15 mL
	2 tbsp	frozen orange juice concentrate	25 mL
	2 tbsp	grated orange peel	25 mL
	3 tbsp	soy sauce	50 mL
	3 tbsp	honey	50 mL
	½ tsp	oriental sesame oil	2 mL

1. Cut off the wing tips and reserve for making stock. Cut the remaining wing in half. (Or wings can be cut into "lollipops" as shown.)

2. Combine all the ingredients for the marinade. Add the wings to the marinade, place in a clean plastic bag, tie securely and marinate for a few hours in the refrigerator, turning the bag occasionally to make sure the wings are well coated.

3. Preheat the oven to 400°F/200°C. Line a baking dish with parchment paper. Arrange the wings in a single layer. Bake for 20 minutes, brush with the marinade, turn wings, brush other side and bake 15 minutes longer. Serve hot or at room temperature.

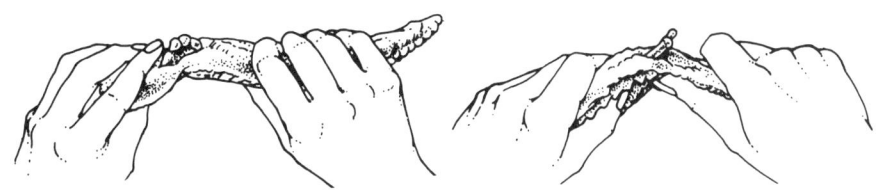

1. Hold the chicken wing parallel to counter with fleshy side down. Grip the "drumstick" section with your left hand and the middle section with your right hand. Force the joint up and pull down sharply with your right hand, exposing the bone of the drumstick. Separate the drumstick from the middle section.

2. Hold the middle section in your left hand and the wing tip in your right hand. Force the joint up and pull down sharply with your right hand, exposing the two thin bones of the middle section. Separate the wing tip from the middle section.

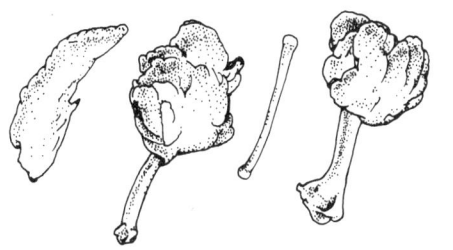

3. Wiggle out the smaller bone from the middle section (it should come free easily). Pull the flesh back from the bone on the middle section and drumstick section, to resemble lollipops. Reserve the wing tips and extra bones and use for stock.

Vegetables with Rouille

Serves 8 to 10

I have always thought that garlic was one of the most delicious flavours in the world. Therefore I am really delighted that it is finally in vogue!

When garlic is cooked for a long time, it becomes gentle and sweet-tasting. When it is used raw, it has a much stronger flavour. In this recipe the garlic flavour is rich and vibrant.

This dip can also be used in fish stews for a last-minute burst of flavour, as a sauce for fish or chicken and as a spread for sandwiches made with cold cuts.

	1 lb	asparagus	500 g
	1	bunch broccoli	1
	1 lb	carrots	500 g
	8 oz	green beans	250 g
	1	large bulb fennel	1
	2	Belgian endives	2
	1	red cabbage	1
ROUILLE	2	cloves garlic	2
	½	red pepper, roasted and peeled (see page 91)	½
	2	egg yolks	2
	¼ tsp	Tabasco sauce (or more to taste)	1 mL
	1 tsp	Dijon mustard	5 mL
	3 tbsp	white wine vinegar	50 mL
	½ tsp	salt	2 mL
	¼ tsp	freshly ground pepper	1 mL
	1 cup	extra-virgin olive oil (or more)	250 mL

1. Break the tough ends off the asparagus. Peel a short way up the stalks. Cook the asparagus in boiling water until tender-crisp, about 3 to 5 minutes. Rinse with cold water and pat dry.

2. Trim the tough ends from the broccoli. Cut into pieces so that the florets are on stems for easier dipping. Cook for 2 to 3 minutes until tender-crisp. Rinse with cold water and pat dry.

3. Peel and trim the carrots and cut into 2-in/5-cm sticks, or cut into carrot flowers as shown. If the carrots are thick, cut them in half. Cook for 3 to 4 minutes until tender-crisp, rinse with cold water and pat dry.

4. Trim the beans. Cook for 2 to 3 minutes until tender-crisp, rinse with cold water and pat dry.

5. Cut the fennel into sticks. Break apart the Belgian endives.

6 Cut the red cabbage in half. Hollow out one half to use as a container for the dip and use the insides and the other half in another recipe.
7 Arrange the vegetables attractively on a large platter.
8 Prepare the rouille by pureeing the garlic and pepper in a blender or food processor.
9 Add the egg yolks, Tabasco, mustard, vinegar, salt, pepper and ¼ cup/50 mL oil. Blend.
10 With the machine running, add the remaining oil slowly through the feed tube until the sauce is thick. Taste and adjust the seasonings if necessary.
11 Spoon the rouille into the hollowed-out cabbage and place in the centre of the vegetables.

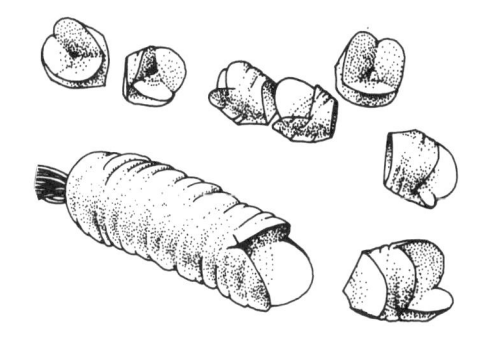

Soups

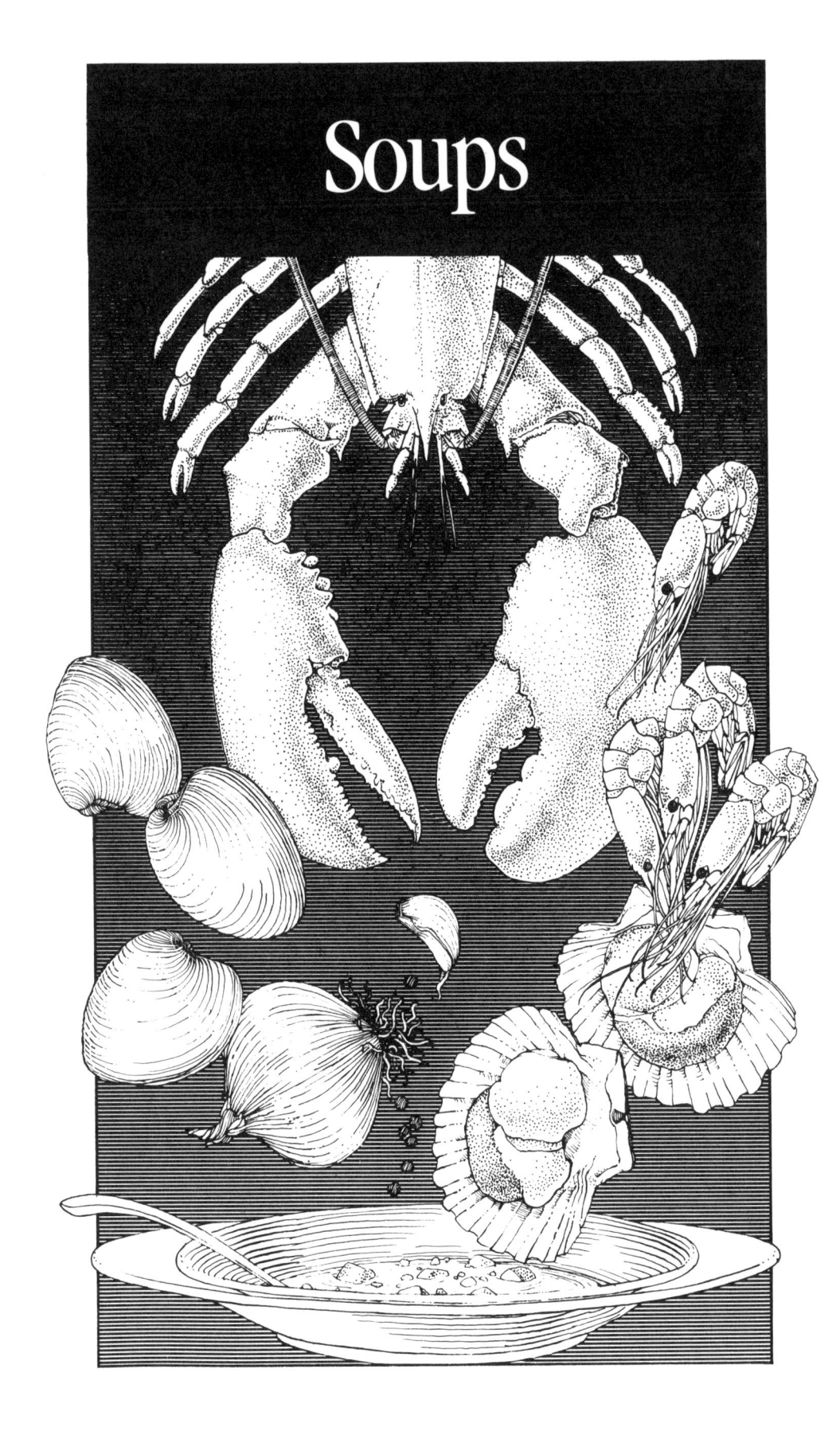

SOUPS

Chicken Soup

Makes approx. 4 qt/4 L

Some people believe that the best chicken soup is made with a kosher chicken. I have discovered that you don't necessarily need a kosher chicken, but it is true that the better the chicken, the better the soup will be. If you want to use the chicken soup in recipes that call for chicken stock, then I usually dilute it a bit to get more mileage out of it.

This soup keeps for about one week in the fridge and a few months in the freezer. The boiled chicken can be used in salads, soups or sandwiches, but most of its flavour will be in the stock.

1	raw chicken, approx. 3 lb/1.5 kg	1
3 qt	cold water	3 L
2	carrots, cut into large chunks	2
2	onions, cut into large chunks	2
2	ribs celery, cut into large chunks	2
2	leeks, cut into large chunks (optional)	2
	Few sprigs fresh parsley	
½ tsp	thyme	2 mL
1	bay leaf	1

1. Cut the chicken into small pieces. Place the chicken, bones, skin, etc. (everything except the liver and giblets, as they tend to discolour the soup) in a large stock pot or Dutch oven. Cover with cold water. Bring to a boil. Skim off any scum that forms on the surface.

2. Add the carrots, onions, celery and leeks. Add the seasonings and reduce the heat. Allow the soup to simmer gently for 1½ to 2 hours.

3. Strain the soup and place it in the refrigerator overnight. All the fat will rise to the surface and solidify, so that it can be removed easily. However, if you intend to keep the soup for a few days, leave the fat on as a protective cover and use the soup from underneath. If you are going to use the soup right away, the best way to remove the fat is to skim it off with a large spoon. Or use a gravy separator. Add salt and pepper to taste as you use the soup.

Scallop and Asparagus Soup

Serves 6 to 8

This is an elegant but low-calorie soup with delicate oriental overtones.

Oriental sesame oil is used as a seasoning, not as a cooking oil. Be sure to buy the flavourful, fragrant, dark sesame oil found in oriental food stores.

2 tbsp	unsalted butter or oil	25 mL
2	cloves garlic, minced	2
2 tsp	minced fresh ginger root	10 mL
2	leeks, sliced	2
4 cups	chicken or fish stock	1 L
1 tbsp	soy sauce	15 mL
½ tsp	oriental sesame oil (optional)	2 mL
8 oz	fresh asparagus	250 g
8 oz	scallops, diced	250 g
3	green onions, sliced	3
	Salt and freshly ground pepper to taste	

1. Melt the butter in a large saucepan and add the garlic, ginger and leeks. Cook for 5 to 10 minutes without browning until the vegetables are very fragrant and tender.

2. Add the stock and bring to a boil. Add the soy sauce and sesame oil. Reduce the heat and simmer gently for 20 minutes.

3. Meanwhile, clean the asparagus and trim off the tough stalks. Peel the stalks a few inches up the stems so they will be more tender. Cut the asparagus into approximately 1-in/2.5-cm pieces. Add to the soup and cook for 5 more minutes. Add the scallops and cook 3 minutes longer.

4. Add the green onions. Taste the soup and season with salt and pepper if necessary. Serve immediately or remove from the heat and reheat very briefly just before serving.

Belgian Endive Soup

Serves 6 to 8

Many people are unfamiliar with the slightly sweet, slightly bitter flavour of Belgian endive. It is wonderful in raw salads but is also delicious cooked in this unusual soup.

3 tbsp	**unsalted butter**	50 mL
3	**leeks, white part only, sliced**	3
5	**Belgian endives, sliced**	5
3	**potatoes, peeled and diced**	3
4 cups	**chicken stock**	1 L
½ tsp	**freshly ground pepper**	2 mL
	Salt to taste	
½ cup	**cream (optional)**	125 mL

1. Melt the butter in large saucepan and add the leeks. Cook until wilted and tender, but do not brown. Add the endives and cook a few minutes longer.

2. Add the potatoes and combine well. Add the stock and pepper and bring to a boil. Cover and cook until tender, about 25 minutes.

3. Puree half the soup in a food processor, blender or food mill, and return to the remaining soup. (If you prefer a completely smooth texture, puree all the soup.) Taste and season with salt if necessary. For a richer version, add ½ cup/125 mL cream after pureeing and heat thoroughly.

Fennel and Leek Soup

Serves 8

Fennel has a slightly anise or licorice flavour. Raw, it can be used in salads or served with dips. Cooked, its flavour becomes more gentle but adds a mysterious, subtle taste. Celery can be used if fennel is unavailable but, of course, the flavour will be quite different.

3 tbsp	unsalted butter	50 mL
3	leeks, thinly sliced	3
3	bulbs fennel, stalks trimmed off, coarsely chopped	3
3 cups	chicken stock	750 mL
1 cup	whipping cream	250 mL
	Salt and freshly ground pepper to taste	

1. Melt the butter in a large saucepan or soup pot. Add the leeks and cook until soft and tender, but do not allow them to brown.
2. Stir in the fennel and continue to cook for 5 minutes.
3. Add the chicken stock and bring to a boil. Reduce the heat, cover and simmer gently for 30 minutes, or until the vegetables are tender.
4. Puree the soup in a blender, food processor or food mill. Return to the saucepan and stir in the cream. Heat thoroughly and add salt and pepper as necessary.

Corn Soup with Herb Cheese

Serves 6 to 8

This is a wonderful way to enjoy fresh corn. The cheese melts and the whole thing is heavenly! If you prefer the soup very smooth, pass it through a food mill after cooking.

	8	ears corn	8
		(or 6 cups/1.5 L frozen niblets)	
	3 tbsp	unsalted butter	50 mL
	1	onion, chopped	1
	1	clove garlic, minced	1
	3 cups	milk	750 mL
		Salt and freshly ground pepper to taste	
	1 cup	cream	250 mL
GARNISH	8 oz	herbed cream cheese (e.g. Boursin or Rondelé)	250 g
	½ cup	chopped fresh parsley or green onions	125 mL

1. Cut the niblets off the ears of corn and process in a blender or food processor. (If using a blender, add up to ½ cup/125 mL water to help blend.)
2. Melt the butter in a large saucepan. Cook the onions and garlic for a few minutes. Add the corn and cook for 5 minutes. Do not brown.
3. Add the milk, bring to a boil, cover and reduce the heat. Simmer for 30 minutes (watch closely to prevent burning). Season with salt and pepper to taste.
4. Stir in the cream and adjust seasoning if necessary. Heat thoroughly.
5. Place 1 oz/30 g cheese in each serving bowl. Spoon in the hot soup and sprinkle with chopped parsley.

Spinach Soup with Dill and Lemon

Serves 6 to 8

Adding rice is a good way to thicken a soup (for people with gluten allergies, this is an especially useful tip). To keep the soup a bright-green colour, do not overcook the spinach and do not cover it while it is cooking.

This soup is also wonderful served hot.

	3 tbsp	unsalted butter	50 mL
	2	onions, finely chopped	2
	1 lb	fresh spinach, washed well, tough stems removed	500 g
	3 tbsp	uncooked rice	50 mL
	1	10-oz/282-g package frozen peas	1
	3 tbsp	chopped fresh dill	50 mL
	4 cups	chicken stock	1 L
		Salt, freshly ground pepper and nutmeg to taste	
		Grated peel of ½ lemon	
	1 cup	whipping cream	250 mL
GARNISH	½ cup	sour cream	125 mL
	8	scallion brushes (see below)	8

1. Melt the butter in a large saucepan and cook the onions until tender.
2. Add the spinach and cook, stirring, until it wilts. Add the rice and peas and toss well. Add the dill.
3. Add the chicken stock and just a little salt, pepper and nutmeg. (These seasonings can be adjusted after the soup is chilled and the flavours blend.) Add the lemon peel. Bring to a boil, reduce the heat and simmer for 20 minutes or until the rice is tender.
4. Puree the soup in a food mill, blender or food processor. Chill.
5. Before serving, stir in the cream. Taste and adjust seasonings.
6. To serve, place a spoonful of sour cream on each serving and float a scallion brush on the sour cream. An alternate garnish is to float paper-thin slices of lemon on the soup.

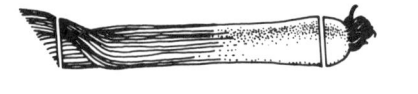

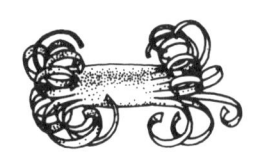

Seafood Chowder

Serves 6 to 8

This is an elegant, rich soup that can be served as an appetizer, or with homemade bread or rolls for a light lunch or supper.

	3 tbsp	unsalted butter	50 mL
	2	onions, finely chopped	2
	1	clove garlic, minced	1
	1 tbsp	all-purpose flour	15 mL
	4 cups	milk or cream (or a combination)	1 L
		Salt and freshly ground pepper to taste	
	½ tsp	thyme	2 mL
	¼ tsp	hot red chili flakes	1 mL
	3	potatoes, diced	3
	8 oz	raw shrimp, coarsely chopped	250 g
	8 oz	raw scallops, coarsely chopped	250 g
	8 oz	raw clams, shucked, or 15-oz/ 200-g tin baby clams (use the liquid as part of the milk in the recipe)	250 g
	8 oz	lobster pieces (if available), or more of any seafood above	250 g
GARNISH		Chopped fresh parsley or chives	

1. Melt the butter in a large pot and cook the onions and garlic, without browning, until tender.

2. Add the flour and cook for a few minutes, also without browning. Stir in the milk and gently bring to a boil (the milk can burn easily). Add the salt, pepper, thyme and hot red chili flakes.

3. Add the potatoes and cook gently, covered, for 30 minutes. (You can partially puree the soup at this point, if you wish.)

4. Add the seafood and cook just a few minutes. Taste and adjust the seasoning if necessary. Serve hot, garnished with parsley or chives.

Cold Cream of Tomato Soup with Basil

Serves 6 to 8

An interesting garnish for this soup is three or four sun-dried tomatoes, cut into julienne strips. Sun-dried tomatoes are dried plum tomatoes, usually packed in olive oil. The best ones have an intense but sweet flavour. If fresh basil is not available, use dill. This soup is also delicious served hot.

	¼ cup	unsalted butter	50 mL
	1	clove garlic, finely chopped	1
	1	onion, finely chopped	1
	1	carrot, finely chopped	1
	¼ cup	all-purpose flour	50 mL
	2 lb	tomatoes, peeled, seeded and chopped	1 kg
	2 tbsp	tomato paste	25 mL
	1	bay leaf	1
	½ tsp	thyme	2 mL
	3 cups	chicken stock	750 mL
		Salt and freshly ground pepper to taste	
	2 tbsp	chopped fresh basil	25 mL
	2 tbsp	chopped fresh parsley	25 mL
	1 cup	whipping cream	250 mL
GARNISH	1 cup	sour cream (preferably Astro)	250 mL
	¼ cup	chopped fresh basil or parsley	50 mL
	2	sun-dried tomatoes, cut in julienne	2

1. Melt the butter in a large pot. Cook the garlic, onions and carrot until tender.
2. Stir in the flour and cook carefully for 5 minutes. Do not brown.
3. Stir in the tomatoes, tomato paste, bay leaf, thyme and chicken stock. Add salt and pepper to taste.
4. Bring to a boil, cover, reduce the heat and cook very gently for 30 minutes. Add the basil and parsley and cook for 1 minute.
5. Puree the mixture in a blender or food processor and chill thoroughly.
6. Just before serving, stir in the cream. Taste and reseason with salt and pepper if necessary. Serve with a dollop of sour cream on top of each serving and sprinkle with basil and sun-dried tomatoes.

Gumbo Ya Ya

Serves 8

Louisiana cooking is so delicious. I have had the pleasure of eating this hearty soup many times in New Orleans. Andouille is a smoked hot sausage found in the south, but Kolbassa is a good substitute. The texture of this soup should be slightly thick and chunky. Serve it over rice in large soup bowls. Filé (feelay) powder is made of ground sassafras leaves and is used as a thickening agent. Add it after the cooking is finished, or it will get stringy. Filé has a fairly pronounced "grassy" flavour and can be found in specialty spice shops.

8 oz	Kolbassa or Andouille sausage, sliced	250 g
½	chicken, skinned, deboned and diced	½
½ cup	vegetable oil	125 mL
½ cup	all-purpose flour	125 mL
2	onions, chopped	2
4	ribs celery, sliced	4
2	red peppers, halved, seeded and diced*	2
2	green peppers, halved, seeded and diced*	2
3	cloves garlic, chopped	3
4 cups	beef or chicken stock	1 L
	Salt and freshly ground pepper to taste	
½ tsp	Tabasco sauce	2 mL
½ tsp	cayenne pepper to taste	2 mL
6	green onions, sliced	6
	Filé powder (optional)	
3 cups	cooked rice	750 mL

1. Cook the sausage and chicken in the oil until slightly browned. Remove, drain and reserve.

2. Remeasure the fat. Place ½ cup/125 mL in a Dutch oven and heat (you may need additional oil). Whisk in the flour and continue to cook carefully over medium-high heat until the roux is dark brown. Be careful not to burn the roux or to splatter yourself (the roux will be very hot).

3. Add the onions, celery, peppers and garlic. Cook for about 5 minutes until slightly wilted. Add the stock and heat.

4. Return the sausage and chicken meat to the pot. Season with salt, pepper, Tabasco and cayenne. Cover and cook gently for 20 minutes.

5. Add the green onions and cook for 10 minutes longer. Season to taste (the soup should be quite spicy). After cooking, you can stir in a little filé powder to thicken the soup more. Do not cook after adding it.

6. Serve over cooked rice.

* *I usually peel the peppers with a vegetable peeler before dicing. This isn't essential, but the peppers will be sweeter.*

Beef and Barley Soup with Wild Mushrooms

Serves 12 to 16

This is a hearty, flavourful, cold-weather soup. It becomes thicker the second day. My mother makes this all the time without the wild mushrooms, and it's great. But the wild mushrooms add a very strong, woodsy flavour.

Although you can make this in a smaller quantity, I usually make the full recipe and freeze the soup to use on different occasions.

2 lb	stewing beef (with bones)	1 kg
3 qt	cold water	3 L
1 oz	dried wild mushrooms	30 g
½ cup	pearl barley	125 mL
2	onions, chopped	2
2	ribs celery, sliced	2
2	carrots, chopped	2
1 tbsp	salt	15 mL
½ tsp	freshly ground pepper	2 mL
1 tsp	thyme	5 mL
1	bay leaf	1
1	clove garlic, minced	1
2 tbsp	chopped fresh parsley	25 mL
1 lb	fresh mushrooms	500 g
1	28-oz/796-mL tin tomatoes	1

1. Combine the meat, bones and water in a large stock pot and bring to a boil. Skim off any scum that rises to the surface. Reduce the heat and simmer for 1 hour.
2. Soak the dried wild mushrooms in 1 cup/250 mL warm water for 20 minutes. Strain the liquid through a paper towel- or cheesecloth-lined strainer to remove the grit or sand. Wash the mushrooms well and chop.
3. Add the dried mushrooms to the soup with the soaking liquid, barley, onions, celery, carrots and seasonings. Cook for another hour.
4. Add the fresh mushrooms and tomatoes. Cook for 30 minutes. Taste and reseason if necessary.

Sweet Red Pepper Soup

Serves 6

Red peppers have become very in vogue. In fact, if there is an "in" colour for the food of the eighties, red is it.

This soup has a wonderful, different flavour. It can also be made with yellow peppers.

	3 tbsp	unsalted butter	50 mL
	1	large red onion, chopped	1
	2	cloves garlic, chopped	2
	¼ tsp	hot red chili flakes	1 mL
	8	large red peppers, halved, seeded and cut into chunks*	8
	2½ cups	chicken stock	625 mL
	¼ tsp	freshly ground pepper	1 mL
		Salt to taste	
	¾ cup	whipping cream	175 mL
GARNISH	3 oz	soft, unripened goat cheese or cream cheese	100 g
	3 tbsp	chopped fresh basil	50 mL

1 Melt the butter in a large saucepan or Dutch oven. Add the onion, garlic and hot chili flakes. Cook for 5 to 8 minutes until tender.

2 Add the red peppers. Combine well and cook for 5 minutes.

3 Add the stock, pepper and salt if necessary. Bring to a boil. Reduce the heat, cover and simmer for 25 minutes.

4 Puree the soup through a food mill and return to the saucepan. Add the cream and heat thoroughly.

5 Serve with a little cheese and basil on top of each serving.

* *A food mill will strain out the pieces of red pepper skin while it is pureeing the soup. If you do not have a food mill, use a blender or food processor, but either peel the peppers (with a vegetable peeler) before cutting or puree and then strain.*

Split Pea Soup with Smoked Ham

Serves 8 to 10

I was thrilled when my school was chosen to be the first Canadian cooking school featured in Bon Appetit *magazine. This delicate version of pea soup, enriched with whipping cream was featured in that article.*

	1 lb	green split peas	500 g
	2 qt	water	2 L
	¼ cup	unsalted butter	50 mL
	3	medium onions, chopped	3
	2	medium cloves garlic, minced	2
	1	rib celery, chopped	1
	2	medium carrots, chopped	2
	4 cups	chicken stock (preferably homemade)	1 L
	8 oz	smoked ham in 1 piece (preferably Black Forest)	250 g
	¼ cup	minced fresh parsley	50 mL
	1 cup	whipping cream	250 mL
		Salt and freshly ground pepper to taste	
GARNISH	4 oz	thinly sliced smoked ham (preferably Black Forest), cut into julienned strips	125 g

1 Soak the peas in the water overnight.

2 Melt the butter in a heavy large saucepan over medium-low heat. Add the onions and garlic and cook until translucent, stirring occasionally, about 10 minutes. Add the celery and carrots and cook for 5 minutes.

3 Drain the peas and rinse. Add them to the pan.

4 Stir in the stock and bring to a boil.

5 Stir in the 8-oz/250-g piece of ham and parsley. Reduce the heat, cover and simmer until the peas are very tender, about 1½ hours.

6 Remove the ham from the soup. Taste the ham and reserve if it is still flavourful. Puree the soup in batches in a food processor or blender. Return to the saucepan and thin with chicken stock or water if necessary.

7 Cut the reserved ham into ½-in/1-cm cubes and return to the soup if desired. Stir in the cream and heat through. Season with salt and pepper.

8 Ladle the soup into bowls. Garnish with the julienned ham and serve. (The soup can be prepared four days ahead. Cover and refrigerate. Thin with chicken stock or water if necessary before serving.)

Pasta e Fagioli

Serves 8

This is a gutsy Italian soup that can be served as an entire meal with crusty bread and a salad. One of my students once left this soup simmering on the stove while she went out shopping for a few hours. When she returned home, the pasta had thickened the soup so much that it had turned into a casserole. Instead of panicking, she poured it into a casserole dish, sprinkled the cheese on top and baked it.

3 tbsp	olive oil or vegetable oil	50 mL
2	onions, chopped	2
3	cloves garlic, minced	3
1	carrot, finely chopped	1
8 oz	boneless pork loin, diced	250 g
¼ tsp	hot red chili flakes	1 mL
3 cups	chicken or beef stock	750 mL
1	28-oz/796-mL tin plum tomatoes	1
1	19-oz/540-g tin cannellini beans	1
8 oz	pasta, in smallish pieces	250 g
	Salt and freshly ground pepper to taste	
1 cup	grated Parmesan cheese (preferably Parmigiano Reggiano)	250 mL

1. Heat the oil in a large saucepan or Dutch oven and cook the onions, garlic and carrot until fragrant. Add the diced pork and chili flakes and cook until the pork is coloured.
2. Add the stock and tomatoes with their juices (break them up slightly) and bring to a boil. Lower the heat, cover and simmer gently for 30 minutes.
3. Rinse the beans under cold water and add to the soup. Cook for 10 minutes.
4. Puree half the soup and return the pureed soup to the pot.
5. Bring the soup to the boil again and add the pasta. Stir to make sure it does not stick on the bottom and cook for 10 minutes, stirring occasionally. If the soup is too thick, add water to thin it.
6. Taste and season with salt and pepper if necessary. Serve sprinkled with Parmesan cheese.

Green Bean Soup with Lemon Chive Butter

Serves 8

The idea for this recipe came from a wonderful cookbook called The Tassajara Recipe Book *by Edward Espe Brown (Shambhala, 1985).*

Any extra lemon and chive butter makes a great "light" version of garlic butter for bread, and it can also be used on veal or lamb chops.

LEMON CHIVE BUTTER

	½ cup	chopped fresh chives or green onions	125 mL
	⅓ cup	unsalted butter	75 mL
		Grated peel of 1 lemon	
		Juice of 1 lemon	
	1	small clove garlic, minced	1
	¼ tsp	salt	1 mL
SOUP	1	onion, chopped	1
	3 tbsp	unsalted butter	50 mL
	1½ lb	green beans, trimmed and chopped	750 g
	4 cups	chicken stock	1 L
	½ tsp	salt (or more to taste)	2 mL
	1 cup	whipping cream	250 mL
		Freshly ground pepper	

1 To make the lemon chive butter, combine the chives, butter, lemon peel, lemon juice, garlic and salt.

2 To make the soup, cook the onion in the butter until tender and fragrant. Add the beans and cook for about 5 minutes.

3 Add the chicken stock and salt. Bring to a boil, reduce the heat and cook until the beans are tender, about 15 minutes.

4 Puree the soup in food processor, blender or food mill. Return to the pot. Add the cream, heat thoroughly and season with pepper. Serve with a spoonful of chive butter on each serving.

Main Courses

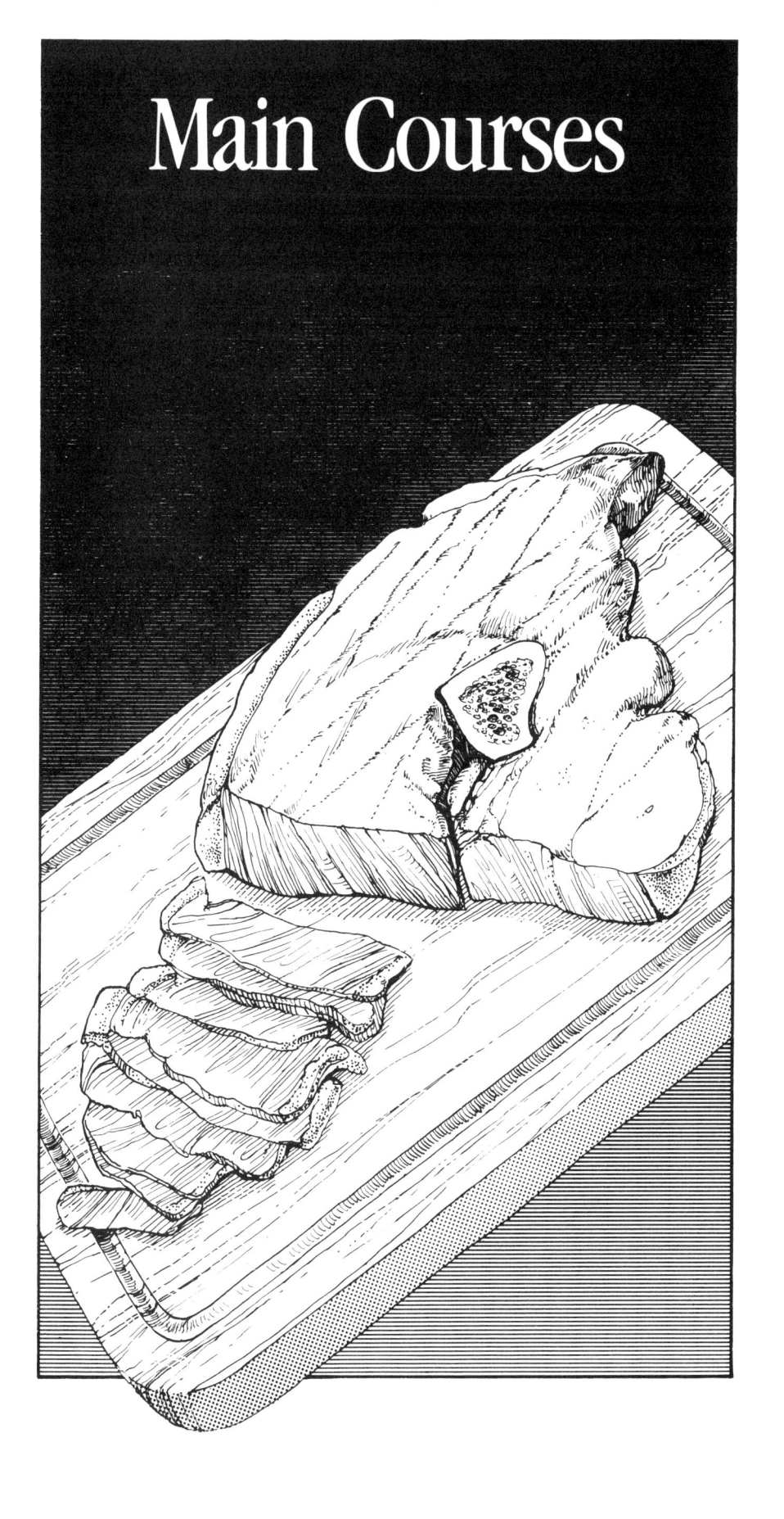

Grilled Tiger Shrimp

Serves 4

Many people tell me that they're afraid to have me over for dinner. But like a lot of people in the food business, I am always thrilled to be invited to someone's home. Rather than being critical, most food people are so aware of the time and energy it takes to cook that they appreciate even the most basic meal.

One of my students, Irene Tam, took the plunge once and did invite me for dinner. The meal was excellent, and these shrimps, served with fresh asparagus, made up just one of the many courses. Irene claims that I taught her everything she knows about cooking, but if I did, she really added her own wonderful style to it all!

12	Tiger shrimps (approx. 2 lb/1 kg)*	12
⅓ cup	lemon juice	75 mL
⅓ cup	extra-virgin olive oil	75 mL
2	cloves garlic, finely chopped	2
½ tsp	salt	2 mL
¼ tsp	freshly ground pepper	1 mL
¼ tsp	hot red chili flakes	1 mL
¼ tsp	dried rosemary (or 1 tbsp/15 mL fresh)	1 mL

1. Using scissors, cut through the shells on the underside of the shrimps. Shell and devein the shrimps. (Or, if you prefer, leave shells on.)

2. Combine the remaining ingredients and pour over the shrimps. Allow to marinate in the refrigerator for a few hours or overnight.

3. When ready to cook, preheat the broiler or barbecue. Cook the shrimps for 3 to 4 minutes on each side or until cooked through.

* *The Tiger shrimps used in this recipe are quite large—2 to 3 oz/60 to 90 g each—and quite expensive. However, this recipe can also be made with smaller shrimps, and in this case I usually cook them on skewers.*

MAIN COURSES

Steamed Salmon and Ginger with Black Bean Sauce

Serves 4

Barbara Klich, "Hour Toronto Magazine's" consumer reporter, secretly loves Chinese food. So this recipe is for her.

You can buy black beans in oriental food markets. They usually come wrapped in plastic and should be stored in the refrigerator after opening.

4	salmon steaks (approx. 6 oz/175 g each)	4
2	slices fresh ginger root, coarsely chopped	2
1 tbsp	rice wine (sake or mirin)	15 mL
1 tsp	salt	5 mL
2 tbsp	peanut oil	25 mL
1 tbsp	fermented black beans, washed, drained and minced	15 mL
2	cloves garlic, chopped	2
1	green onion, chopped	1
1 tsp	minced fresh ginger root	5 mL
¼ cup	chicken stock or water	50 mL
1 tbsp	soy sauce	15 mL
1 tbsp	rice wine (sake or mirin)	15 mL

1 Rinse the salmon steaks and pat them dry. Place in a bowl.

2 Combine the ginger, 1 tbsp/15 mL rice wine, and salt and sprinkle on the salmon. Allow to marinate for 15 minutes.

3 Discard the raw ginger and place the salmon in a single layer in an ovenproof flat dish with a rim.

4 Heat the oil in a wok or skillet and add the beans, garlic, green onion and minced ginger. Stir fry until very fragrant (about 10 seconds) and then add the stock, soy sauce and 1 tbsp/15 mL rice wine. Cook for 2 minutes, stirring constantly. Pour the sauce over the fish.

5 Place a steamer rack (or four criss-crossed chopsticks, as shown) in the bottom of the wok. Fill to the bottom of the rack with water. Heat until boiling. Place the dish of fish on the rack and cover. Steam over high heat for 10 to 15 minutes or just until the fish is cooked. If the water in the wok evaporates too quickly, add some boiling water. Serve immediately. (If you do not have a wok, cover an ovenproof baking dish with foil and bake in the oven at 400°F/200°C for 10 to 15 minutes.)

Stir-fried Scallops with Broccoli

Serves 6

When I went to Taiwan to take cooking classes, I was dismayed to learn that in most restaurants, the meat and sometimes even the vegetables in stir-fried dishes are deep-fried first. However, in home-style Chinese dishes such as this one, this isn't always so. Not only is this recipe quick and delicious—it's also low in calories.

1½ lb	fresh scallops	750 g
2	slices ginger root, smashed	2
2	green onions, smashed	2
2 tbsp	rice wine	25 mL
1	bunch broccoli, trimmed, with the tough skin removed (about 1 lb/500 g)	1
2 tbsp	peanut oil	25 mL
12	1-in/2.5-cm pieces green onion	12
1 tsp	minced fresh ginger root	5 mL
2	cloves garlic, minced	2
SAUCE ½ cup	chicken stock	125 mL
1 tsp	salt	5 mL
2 tbsp	rice wine	25 mL
½ tsp	sugar	2 mL
1 tsp	oriental sesame oil	5 mL
2 tsp	cornstarch	10 mL

1. Rinse the scallops and drain them well. Slice each in half horizontally and place in a bowl.

2. Add the smashed ginger root and green onions to 2 tbsp/25 mL rice wine (this allows the flavours to go into the wine). Then discard the ginger and onions and combine the scallops with the wine. Toss lightly and allow them to marinate for 30 minutes.

3. Meanwhile, slice the broccoli stems on the diagonal. Separate the florets. Cook the broccoli in boiling water for 3 minutes. Refresh under cold water to stop the cooking and set the colour. Pat dry and reserve.

4. Combine all the ingredients for the sauce.

5. Heat a wok or a large skillet. Add the peanut oil. Heat the oil until very hot and add the pieces of green onion, minced ginger root and garlic. Stir-fry until fragrant.

6. Add the broccoli and sauce to the wok and toss well. Add the scallops. When the sauce has thickened and the scallops are just cooked, about 2 minutes, remove to a platter and serve with steamed rice.

Sole with Lemon and Capers

Serves 4

This lightly battered fish dish is fast and easy to prepare. It's so delicious that it's sure to make fish a family favourite. It also works well with salmon fillets or any thin fillet—it's even great with thin veal scallops.

4	sole fillets (approx. 4 oz/125 g each)	4
	Salt and freshly ground pepper	
1 cup	all-purpose flour	250 mL
2	eggs	2
⅓ cup	unsalted butter	75 mL
⅓ cup	lemon juice	75 mL
2 tbsp	capers	25 mL
2 tbsp	unsalted butter	25 mL
¼ tsp	freshly ground pepper	1 mL
¼ cup	chopped fresh parsley	50 mL

1. Pat the fish dry with paper towels and season lightly with salt and pepper. Place the eggs in a flat dish and beat them together.

2. Dip the fillets into the flour and shake off the excess. Dip the floured fish into the eggs to coat. Redip the fish into the flour.

3. Heat ⅓ cup/75 mL butter in a large skillet and cook the fish about 3 minutes on each side (cook in two batches if necessary). Remove to a serving platter and keep warm while preparing the sauce.

4. Discard any excess fat that remains in the skillet. Return the skillet to the heat and add the lemon juice and capers. Deglaze the pan by scraping up any bits of solidified juices and combining them into the sauce. Remove from the heat and add 2 tbsp/25 mL butter, ¼ tsp/1 mL pepper and the parsley. Pour over the fish and serve immediately.

Lemon Salmon Teriyaki

Serves 6

This is a special treat during barbecue season, but also works beautifully under the broiler. The skin gets black and crispy—it's my favourite part.

½ cup	soy sauce	125 mL
⅓ cup	sugar	75 mL
¼ cup	rice wine or sake	50 mL
1	clove garlic, minced	1
1 tsp	minced fresh ginger root	5 mL
	Juice of 1 lemon	
1 tsp	dry mustard	5 mL
6	salmon steaks or fillets (approx. 6 oz/175 g each)	6

1. Combine all the ingredients except the salmon steaks and bring to a boil. Cook for a few minutes until syrupy.
2. Barbecue or broil the salmon steaks (about 5 minutes on each side if steaks are about 1 in/2.5 cm thick). Brush with the glaze a few times on each side during cooking.

Whisky-glazed Steak

Serves 4

When Judy Webb goes on vacation, I sometimes do the show with Dave Agar. If you listen to the show, you'll know that Dave is a serious news type, and cooking is not always at the top of his mind. However, when it comes to barbecued steak, I can usually catch his interest. This recipe is different, fast and easy.

1 tbsp	Worcestershire sauce	15 mL
½ tsp	Tabasco sauce	2 mL
3 tbsp	dry mustard	50 mL
2 tbsp	whisky (or more)	25 mL
4	steaks (New York sirloins, filets or rib—approx. 8 oz/250 g each)	4

1. Make a paste with the Worcestershire sauce, Tabasco sauce, mustard and whisky. Add more whisky or mustard if needed, but the paste should be pretty thick.

2. Smear the paste all over the steaks and allow to marinate at room temperature for 30 minutes.

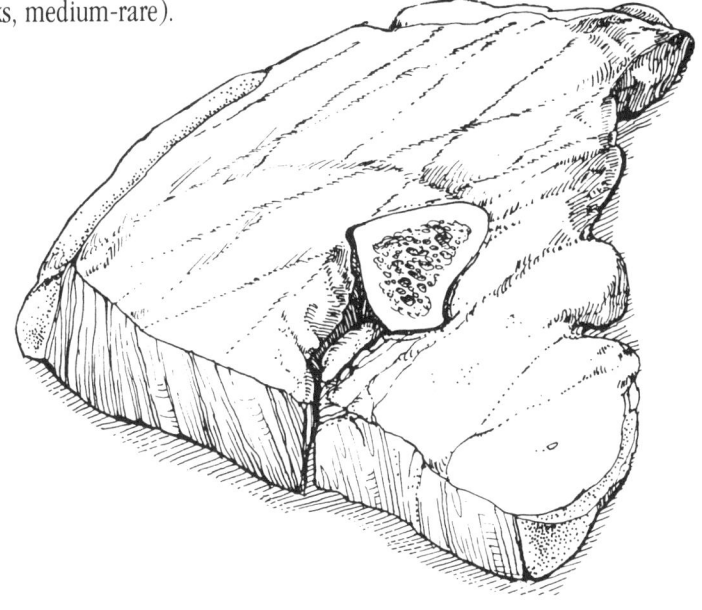

3. Barbecue or broil the steaks for 3 to 4 minutes per side (to cook 1-in/2.5-cm thick steaks, medium-rare).

Marinated Flank Steak

Serves 4 to 6

"Hour Toronto Magazine's" money man Brian Costello would approve of this recipe for flank steak, a delicious but less expensive cut. When the meat is marinated, it becomes more tender and barbecues or broils beautifully. This steak is also delicious served cold.

⅓ cup	white wine vinegar	75 mL
⅓ cup	Balsamic vinegar	75 mL
⅓ cup	olive oil	75 mL
1	clove garlic, minced	1
2 tbsp	Dijon mustard	25 mL
1 tbsp	Worcestershire sauce	15 mL
1 tsp	salt	5 mL
¼ tsp	freshly ground pepper	1 mL
1	bay leaf	1
½ tsp	thyme	2 mL
1	flank steak (approx. 1½ lb/750 g)	1

1 Combine all the ingredients except for the steak. Place in a plastic bag and add the steak. Massage the marinade into the steak and press out any air in the bag. Tie securely. Place in the refrigerator and marinate the meat overnight.

2 Heat the barbecue or broiler. Brush the grill with oil and heat.

3 Remove the meat from the marinade and pat dry. Place on the hot grill and cook for 5 to 6 minutes per side for rare. Slice very thinly, on the diagonal.

MAIN COURSES

Steak with Mustard Cream Sauce *Serves 2*

This makes a terrific fast dinner. The recipe also works well with chicken breasts or veal chops. Double or triple the recipe for four or six people.

2	thin New York sirloins or boneless rib steaks (or any other tender cut) approx. 6 oz/175 g each	2
	Vegetable oil	
1	shallot, chopped	1
½ cup	dry white wine	125 mL
2 tbsp	Dijon mustard	25 mL
⅓ cup	whipping cream	75 mL
½ tsp	Worcestershire sauce	2 mL
	Salt and freshly ground pepper to taste	

1. Pat the steaks dry with paper towels.
2. Brush a skillet with oil and heat. Add the steaks and cook about 3 to 4 minutes on each side for a medium-rare 1-in/2.5-cm steak. Remove the steaks to serving plates. Discard any excess fat in the pan.
3. Return the pan to the heat and add the shallots and wine. Cook over medium-high heat, scraping the bottom to loosen any bits of solidified juices stuck to the pan. Reduce the liquid to a few tablespoons.
4. Stir in the mustard and then add the cream. Cook until slightly thickened and taste. Add the Worcestershire sauce and salt and pepper if necessary. Pour the sauce over the steaks and serve.

Steaks with Green Peppercorn Sauce

Serves 4

Green peppercorns are unripe peppercorn berries, and they are much milder than traditional black or white peppercorns (they are available in specialty stores). This sauce also works well with veal chops.

4	**New York sirloins or filets** approx. 6 oz/175 g each)	4
2 tbsp	**vegetable oil**	25 mL
⅔ cup	**dry white or red wine**	150 mL
3 tbsp	**Cognac**	50 mL
½ tsp	**Dijon mustard**	2 mL
2 tbsp	**crushed green peppercorns**	25 mL
¾ cup	**whipping cream**	175 mL
2 tbsp	**chopped fresh parsley**	25 mL

1. Preheat the oven to 200°F/90°C.
2. Dry the steaks well with paper towels. Heat the oil in a heavy skillet and cook the steaks until they are a little less done than you want them in the end. (A steak that is 1 in/2.5 cm thick will require approximately 3 to 4 minutes on each side for medium-rare.)
3. Remove the steaks to a serving platter and keep them warm in the oven. Discard any excess fat from the pan and return the pan to the heat.
4. Add the wine to the pan and deglaze by scraping the bits of solidified juices off the bottom of the pan and into the sauce. Add the Cognac. Cook until the liquid is reduced by half and slightly thickened.
5. Add the mustard and peppercorns and cook for a few minutes longer. Press the peppercorns with the back of a spoon. Stir in the cream. Bring to a boil and reduce until slightly thickened.
6. Pour the sauce over the steaks and sprinkle with parsley.

Blackened Sirloin Steak

Serves 8

This is in the style of Cajun cooking. It is hot, spicy and wonderful. Many different kinds of peppers are used in this mix, but they all add their own particular flavour. Because the spice mix creates a lot of smoke when cooking, it is best to do this outdoors on a barbecue.

1 tbsp	**freshly ground white pepper**	15 mL
1 tbsp	**freshly ground black pepper**	15 mL
1 tbsp	**salt**	15 mL
1 tbsp	**dry mustard**	15 mL
1 tbsp	**paprika**	15 mL
2 tsp	**cayenne pepper**	10 mL
¼ tsp	**dried ground fennel (optional)**	1 mL
½ tsp	**thyme**	2 mL
½ tsp	**oregano**	2 mL
⅓ cup	**unsalted butter**	75 mL
2	**cloves garlic, minced**	2
2½ lb	**sirloin steak (approx. 1½ in/4 cm thick)**	1.5 kg

1 Combine all the dry spices for the seasoning mix.
2 Melt the butter and combine with the garlic.
3 When you are ready to cook the steak, dip it into the garlic butter and then pat the seasonings into each side.
4 Preheat the barbecue and brush the grill with oil. Barbecue the steak for 7 to 10 minutes on each side for rare, depending on the thickness of the steak. The steak will "blacken," so do not worry. Also, a lot of smoke will be created by the seasoning mix. Douse the flames with water if necessary.

MAIN COURSES

Mustard-glazed Sirloin Steak

Serves 8

Barbecued sirloin steak, carved into thin slices on the diagonal, reminds me of a mini roast, where every slice has a great barbecue flavour. If it is not barbecue season, broil it.

This "cow" recipe is for Don Daynard, our meat and potatoes movie buff.

1	2-lb/1-kg sirloin steak (approx. 1½ in/4 cm thick)	1
⅓ cup	Dijon mustard	75 mL
2 tbsp	olive oil	25 mL
2 tbsp	lemon juice	25 mL
1 tbsp	Worcestershire sauce	15 mL
½ tsp	Tabasco sauce	2 mL
½ tsp	freshly ground pepper	2 mL
1 tbsp	soy sauce	15 mL

1. Pat the steak dry.

2. Combine the remaining ingredients and spread the mixture on both sides of the steak. Allow to marinate in the refrigerator for 30 minutes, or up to 3 hours.

3. Preheat the barbecue or broiler. Brush the grill with a little oil and heat before placing the steak on it (this will prevent sticking). Cook for 7 to 10 minutes per side for medium-rare. Allow the steak to rest for 5 minutes before carving. Slice on the diagonal.

MAIN COURSES

Barbecued Brisket

Serves 6 to 8

This brisket is actually roasted in the oven, though it has a hot, spicy, barbecued flavour. It is easy and quick to prepare but should bake for a long time so that the meat becomes very tender. I prefer a double brisket because it is juicier, but it does contain more fat.

1	5-lb/2.5-kg brisket	1
3	onions, sliced	3
1 cup	ketchup	250 mL
½ cup	chili sauce	125 mL
1 cup	water	250 mL
1	4-oz/110-g tin chopped green chilies	1
¼ cup	Dijon mustard	50 mL
2 tbsp	vinegar	25 mL
1 tbsp	Worcestershire sauce	15 mL
1 tsp	Tabasco sauce	5 mL
½ tsp	freshly ground pepper	2 mL
2	cloves garlic, minced	2

1. Preheat the oven to 350°F/180°C.
2. Pat the brisket dry. Place the onions in the bottom of a roasting pan and sit the brisket on top.
3. Combine the remaining ingredients and pour over the top of the meat.
4. Cover tightly and roast for 3½ hours. Every hour, remove the lid and add additional water if the pan is getting dry. There should always be at least 1 cup/250 mL liquid in the bottom of the pan.
5. After 3½ hours, remove the lid and return to the oven for 20 to 30 minutes until brown.

Spicy Burgers

Serves 8

For a surprise in hamburgers, try these. They are juicy and really delicious.

Hamburgers will all cook at the same time (even if they are different weights) if they are the same thickness. So, if your family is of various weights and sizes, vary the weight of the burger but not the thickness.

2 lb	ground beef	1 kg
½ cup	hot taco sauce (use mild if you wish)	125 mL
1	egg	1
2	cloves garlic, minced	2
1 tsp	chili powder	5 mL
1	small onion, finely chopped	1
½ cup	fresh breadcrumbs	125 mL
	Salt and freshly ground pepper to taste	

1 Combine all the ingredients together well. Shape into eight patties.
2 Barbecue or pan fry about 8 minutes on each side for medium. Turn them carefully.

MAIN COURSES

Deviled Chicken

Serves 4

This is a simple preparation, so start with a really good-quality chicken. You can make it more "devilish" by adding Tabasco, pepper and chili flakes. The chicken can also be broiled.

½ cup	extra-virgin olive oil	125 mL
¼ cup	lemon juice	50 mL
2 tbsp	Dijon mustard	25 mL
1 tsp	Tabasco sauce	5 mL
½ tsp	salt	2 mL
½ tsp	freshly ground pepper	2 mL
½ tsp	dried rosemary (or 1 tbsp/15 mL fresh)	2 mL
¼ tsp	hot dried chili flakes	1 mL
1	chicken, cut into serving pieces (approx. 4 lb/2 kg)	1

1. Combine the oil, lemon juice, mustard, Tabasco sauce, salt, pepper, rosemary and chili flakes. Taste and correct seasoning.
2. Rub the mixture into the chicken and allow it to marinate for 30 minutes.
3. Barbecue the chicken skin side down for 10 minutes. Then turn and cook for 15 to 20 minutes until the juices run yellow when pierced at the joint. Baste with extra marinade during the cooking.

Apricot-glazed Chicken

Serves 4 to 6

This flavourful recipe is fast and easy, but makes a dinner taste very special. The chicken is perfect served hot, but is also great cold for picnics.

1	chicken (approx. 4 lb/2 kg)	1
½ cup	apricot jam	125 mL
2 tbsp	Dijon mustard	25 mL
2 tbsp	soy sauce	25 mL
1 tsp	Worcestershire sauce	5 mL
½ tsp	Tabasco sauce	2 mL
1	clove garlic, minced	1
1 tsp	minced fresh ginger root	5 mL

1. Preheat the oven to 375°F/190°C.

2. Cut the chicken into 4 or 6 pieces. Pat dry. Place the chicken skin side up on a jelly roll pan lined with aluminum foil or parchment paper.

3. Combine the remaining ingredients in a small saucepan and cook until well blended, about 2 to 3 minutes.

4. Brush the glaze on the chicken. Bake for 40 to 50 minutes or until the chicken is just cooked through. Baste occasionally.

Chicken with Raspberry Vinegar *Serves 6*

This is stunning in appearance and flavour. It is also easy and quick to prepare and low in calories. In short—perfect!

You can use sherry vinegar, white or red wine vinegar, or any herb vinegar instead of the raspberry vinegar. You can also use your favourite herb, fresh or dried, instead of rosemary.

Serve this with a rice pilaf.

3	chicken breasts, split, skinned and boned	3
	All-purpose flour	
3 tbsp	unsalted butter	50 mL
	Salt and freshly ground pepper to taste	
½ tsp	dried rosemary (or 2 tbsp/25 mL fresh)	2 mL
⅓ cup	raspberry vinegar	75 mL
2 tbsp	unsalted butter	25 mL
4 oz	snow peas	125 g
1 lb	cherry tomatoes	500 g

1. Preheat the oven to 200°F/90°C.
2. Remove the "filets" from the chicken breasts and cut in half across the middle. Slice the remaining piece of chicken into 6 pieces.
3. Shake the chicken strips with flour in a large sieve over a bowl (so that the excess flour gets sifted away).
4. In a large skillet, heat 3 tbsp/50 mL butter. Add the chicken pieces and cook, stirring constantly, until cooked through. This should not take too long as the pieces are small and breast meat is very tender. While the chicken is cooking, season with salt, pepper and rosemary. (You may have to cook the chicken in two batches.)
5. Remove the chicken to a serving platter and keep warm in the oven.
6. Discard any fat left in the skillet and return to medium heat. Add the vinegar and cook until it is reduced to a few tablespoons. Scrape the bottom of the pan to remove any bits of chicken (this deglazing will add a lot of flavour to the sauce). Pour the sauce over the chicken.
7. Return the pan to the heat and add 2 tbsp/25 mL butter. Add the snow peas and cook for 2 minutes. Add the cherry tomatoes and cook just until heated through. Season with salt and pepper. Arrange around the outside edge of the chicken for a garnish.

Voodoo Chicken with Cornbread Stuffing

Serves 6

Cajun cooking has become so popular that people are blackening everything. I think I have even heard of a blackened cheesecake! This lightly blackened chicken breast is superb. It is best to barbecue the chicken outdoors, because it smokes a lot, but do not overcook it—the outside should be spicy and crisp and the inside should be juicy and tender. Be sure to serve it with the cornbread stuffing.

	CORNBREAD STUFFING	
¼ cup	unsalted butter	50 mL
2	red onions, chopped	2
3	cloves garlic, minced	3
2	ribs celery, chopped	2
2	red peppers, peeled seeded and chopped	2
1	green pepper, peeled seeded and chopped	1
1	4-oz/110-g tin chopped green chilies	1
1 tsp	chili powder	5 mL
½ tsp	salt (or more to taste)	2 mL
¼ tsp	freshly ground black pepper	1 mL
¼ tsp	freshly ground white pepper	1 mL
4 cups	diced cornbread (see page 113)	1 L
2	eggs, lightly beaten	2
½ cup	cream or sour cream (preferably Astro)	125 mL
VOODOO CHICKEN		
3	large whole chicken breasts, split and boned but with the skin left on (each boned piece of chicken should weigh about 5 oz/150 g)	3
¼ cup	unsalted butter, melted	50 mL
3	cloves garlic, minced	3
2 tsp	freshly ground black pepper	10 mL
2 tsp	freshly ground white pepper	10 mL
2 tsp	paprika	10 mL
½ tsp	cayenne pepper	2 mL
1 tsp	dry mustard	5 mL
¼ tsp	thyme	1 mL
¼ tsp	oregano	1 mL
1	small piece bay leaf, crushed	1
1 tsp	salt	5 mL

1. To prepare the stuffing, melt the butter in a large skillet and add the onions and garlic. Cook until tender and fragrant.

2. Add the celery, peppers and chilies. Cook for a few minutes until the vegetables are very tender. Season with chili powder, salt, black and white pepper and toss with the cornbread. Taste and adjust seasonings if necessary.

3 Stir in the eggs and cream. If you are cooking the stuffing on the barbecue, brush a large piece of foil with butter, place the stuffing in the centre and wrap to form a tight package. Barbecue for about 20 minutes per side. (If you are oven-baking the stuffing, place in a buttered 3-qt/3-L casserole dish and bake at 375°F/190°C for 30 to 40 minutes or until the top is browned.)
4 To prepare the chicken, pat the chicken breasts dry. Combine the melted butter and garlic and place in a flat dish. Dip pieces of chicken in the garlic-butter mixture so that both sides are coated. Allow to marinate until ready to cook.
5 Combine all the remaining ingredients. Just before cooking, sprinkle this spice mixture evenly over both sides of the chicken and pat in slightly.
6 Barbecue the chicken for approximately 5 to 7 minutes per side, skin side first, until just barely cooked.

Chinese Emerald Chicken

Serves 6

This is also good made with pork tenderloin, chicken livers or shrimps. Serve it with rice for a complete meal.

2 tbsp	vegetable oil	25 mL
2	chicken breasts, split, skinned boned and cut into chunks	2
1 tbsp	finely chopped ginger root	15 mL
1	onion, sliced	1
1	green pepper, diced	1
8 oz	broccoli, chopped	250 g
2	stalks celery, sliced	2
4 oz	snow peas	125 g
	Salt and freshly ground pepper	
½ cup	chicken stock	125 mL
2 tbsp	soy sauce	25 mL
1 tbsp	rice wine	15 mL
1 tbsp	cornstarch	15 mL
¼ cup	water	50 mL
1 tbsp	toasted sesame seeds	15 mL

1 Heat the oil in a wok.

2 Dry the chicken pieces well and add to the wok with the ginger. Stir and cook until the chicken whitens.

3 Stir in the onions and cook for a few minutes. Add the remaining vegetables and cook a few minutes longer. Season with salt and pepper.

4 Add the stock, soy sauce and wine. Cover and cook until the liquid comes to a boil. Cook for 2 minutes. Reduce the heat and cook gently for 2 to 3 minutes.

5 Combine the cornstarch with the water and stir until smooth. Increase the heat. Mix into vegetables and cook until just thickened. Sprinkle with sesame seeds.

Marmalade-glazed Leg of Lamb *Serves 6*

Whenever I think of the birth of my daughter, Anna, I think of this leg of lamb. I was cooking it just as I had the first suspicion of labour. And my doctor husband, Ray, wouldn't let me eat any of it, just in case. He was right, of course, as Anna was born just two hours later, but it was the first barbecue of the season and the lamb was pink and juicy and smelled just wonderful. I really was craving some. When my good friends Jim and Carol White heard this story, they were sympathetic. As parents of two children themselves, Jenny and Jason, they knew I had probably received enough flowers and baby sleepers. So they sent me a leg of lamb! It was the most thoughtful and original present ever given to a new mother.

	1	leg of lamb, butterflied (approx. 4 lb/2 kg after boning)	1
	1 tbsp	vegetable oil	15 mL
GLAZE	½ cup	marmalade	125 mL
	1 tbsp	minced fresh ginger root	15 mL
	1	clove garlic, minced	1
	¼ cup	Dijon mustard	50 mL
	2 tbsp	soy sauce (preferably dark)	25 mL
	1 tsp	Worcestershire sauce	5 mL
	½ tsp	Tabasco sauce	2 mL

1. Pat the lamb dry and flatten out as much as possible. Remove any excess fat. Brush lightly with the oil.
2. Preheat the barbecue or broiler.
3. Combine the ingredients for the glaze and heat.
4. Cook the lamb 15 minutes per side for rare. Brush with the glaze a few times during cooking. Allow the lamb to rest for 5 to 10 minutes before carving. Slice thinly.

Lemon Mint Lamb Chops

Serves 4

Compound butters were once a chef's secret. But they are so easy to prepare, look so good and taste so terrific that they are a trick well worth learning. They can be made with a multitude of seasonings and served on any plain cooked meat or fish.

8	loin lamb chops	8
3 tbsp	lemon juice	50 mL
½ tsp	salt	2 mL
3 tbsp	extra-virgin olive oil	50 mL
1 tbsp	chopped fresh mint (or ½ tsp/2 mL dried)	15 mL
	Freshly ground pepper	
LEMON MINT BUTTER		
½ cup	unsalted butter	125 mL
2 tbsp	lemon juice	25 mL
1 tbsp	chopped fresh mint (or ½ tsp/2 mL dried)	15 mL
	Salt and freshly ground pepper to taste	

1. Trim the lamb chops of all but a little excess fat. Combine the lemon juice, salt, olive oil, mint and pepper. Marinate the lamb in this mixture in a flat dish, turning often, for at least 30 minutes at room temperature or longer in the refrigerator.

2. While lamb is marinating, prepare the compound butter. Cream the butter with the lemon juice, mint and salt and pepper to taste. Place the butter on a piece of waxed paper and shape into a cylinder about 3 in x 1½ in/7.5 cm x 3.5 cm. Refrigerate.

3. Broil, barbecue or pan fry the lamb chops approximately 3 to 5 minutes on each side (they should be slightly rare). Slice the butter thinly and place two slices on each hot chop. The butter will melt slowly and moisten and flavour the lamb.

Provimi Veal Liver

Serves 4 to 6

This is one of the most sensational ways I have ever had liver. The peppercorns match the flavour of the liver and have even converted some students into liver lovers. Provimi liver is the most delicate and the most expensive, but this dish is also great with calves' liver.

1½ lb	Provimi veal liver, sliced ½ in/1 cm thick	750 g
1 cup	all-purpose flour	250 mL
2	eggs	2
3 cups	fresh breadcrumbs	750 mL
2 tbsp	crushed black peppercorns	25 mL
1 tsp	salt	5 mL
¼ cup	unsalted butter	50 mL
GARNISH	**Thin lemon slices**	

1. Remove any skin from the liver. If necessary, cut into serving pieces (sometimes the liver is cut in long slices, which would be too much for one serving. Each serving should be 4 to 5 oz/125 to 150 g).

2. Have on hand a plate of flour, another plate with the beaten eggs in it and another plate of breadcrumbs combined with the peppercorns and salt. Pat the liver dry with paper towels and then dust with flour. Dip into the egg to coat well and then into the crumbs. Pat the crumbs into the liver firmly and set on a rack to dry. Refrigerate until ready to cook.

3. In a large heavy skillet, melt the butter. Cook the liver on medium heat for 4 to 5 minutes on each side. The crumbs should be crisp but not too brown and the liver should be medium-rare. Garnish with lemon slices.

Veal Scaloppine with Marsala Cream Sauce

Serves 3 to 4

Although all Marsala wine is "sweet," when you cook with it, be sure to use the driest version you can find. This recipe also works beautifully with veal chops or chicken breasts.

2 tbsp	vegetable oil	25 mL
¼ cup	unsalted butter	50 mL
1 lb	thin veal scallops	500 g
½ cup	all-purpose flour	125 mL
½ cup	dry Marsala	125 mL
⅓ cup	whipping cream	75 mL
	Salt and freshly ground pepper to taste	

1. Heat the oil and butter in a large skillet.
2. Dredge the scallops in the flour and add to the pan (you may have to do this in two batches).
3. Brown the scallops quickly on both sides (a minute or so each side). When they are brown, transfer them to a platter and keep warm.
4. Pour off any fat remaining in the pan and return to the heat. Add the Marsala.
5. Scrape the bottom of the pan, stir, and add the cream. Stir constantly over high heat until the sauce thickens a little. Season with salt and pepper to taste. Pour the sauce over the scallops.

Western Barbecued Pork Chops *Serves 6*

This is a great way to have pork chops. Tender chops can be used, but butt chops, which are often less tender and less expensive, work especially well—they become moist and juicy when marinated and cooked this way.

If there is extra marinade and you want to use it as a sauce, cook the marinade for 5 to 10 minutes, uncovered, until it thickens slightly. If you do not like a very spicy sauce, cut down on the Tabasco, hot chili flakes, mustard and chilies.

	3	butt pork chops (approx. 1½ lb/750 g each)	3
MARINADE	1½ cups	barbecue sauce or ketchup	375 mL
	1 tbsp	Worcestershire sauce	25 mL
	1 tsp	Tabasco sauce	5 mL
	¼ tsp	hot red chili flakes	1 mL
	2 tbsp	Dijon mustard	25 mL
	¼ cup	honey	50 mL
	¼ cup	lemon juice or vinegar	50 mL
	2	onions, finely chopped	2
	3	cloves garlic, minced	3
	1	yellow banana pepper, chopped	1
	½ cup	ketchup	125 mL

1. Place the pork chops in a large plastic bag.
2. Combine all the ingredients for the marinade and pour into the bag with the chops. Seal. Marinate in the refrigerator overnight.
3. Prepare the barbecue. When the coals are covered with a grey ash, barbecue the chops. If they are approximately 1 in/2.5 cm thick, they will take 15 to 20 minutes on each side. Baste with the marinade as they cook. Be careful, as they could burn easily. These can also be baked in the oven at 375°F/190°C for 30 minutes per side.

Sweet and Sour Spareribs

Serves 4 to 6

People are often thrown off by the idea of cooking a Chinese meal. For some reason they think all the dishes have to be stir-fried. In traditional banquet-style meals, however, many different cooking methods are used. This dish is great served as part of a Chinese meal. Because the ribs are braised, they can be made ahead and reheated. Or they can be served with rice as a main course on their own.

3 lb	spareribs, split down the centre lengthwise by the butcher	1.5 kg
1	piece ginger root, smashed	1
2	green onions, cut in large pieces and smashed	2
1 tsp	salt	5 mL
2 tsp	rice wine	10 mL
1½ tsp	soy sauce	7 mL
4 cups	vegetable oil for deep frying (more if necessary)	1 L
1 tsp	minced ginger root	5 mL
1 tbsp	minced garlic	15 mL
½ cup	ketchup	125 mL
4 cups	chicken stock or water	1 L
¼ cup	sugar	50 mL
1 tsp	salt	5 mL
1½ tsp	rice vinegar	7 mL
1 tsp	oriental sesame oil	5 mL

1. Cut the ribs into individual pieces.
2. Combine the smashed ginger, smashed green onions, 1 tsp/5 mL salt, rice wine and soy sauce. Place in a bowl with the ribs and toss well. Allow to marinate for at least 30 minutes. Discard the ginger and green onions and pat ribs dry.
3. Heat a wok and add the vegetable oil for deep frying. Heat the oil. Deep-fry the ribs for about 5 minutes, in batches if necessary, or until well browned. Drain well. (The ribs can also be browned under the broiler.)
4. Remove all but 2 tbsp/25 mL oil from the wok. Reheat. Add the minced ginger and garlic and cook until fragrant.
5. Add the ketchup, chicken stock, sugar, 1 tsp/5 mL salt and vinegar. Bring to a boil and return the ribs to the wok.
6. Cover the pan and cook the ribs on medium-high heat for approximately 30 minutes. Remove the cover and cook on high heat, stirring constantly, until the ribs are well glazed and almost all the liquid has evaporated (this may take 10 to 15 minutes).
7. Sprinkle the ribs with the sesame oil and serve immediately.

Chinese Barbecued Ribs

Serves 6

Ken Day loves ribs, so whenever I do the show with him, I try to tempt him with one of the dozens of delicious rib recipes that I know.

I have always thought the secret of tender ribs is to precook them. That way they do not dry out or burn from sugary sauces.

4 lb	back or side ribs	2 kg
½ cup	ketchup	125 mL
½ cup	Hoisin sauce	125 mL
3	cloves garlic, minced	3
1 tbsp	minced ginger root	15 mL
1 tbsp	hot Chinese chili sauce or paste	15 mL
3 tbsp	soy sauce	50 mL
1 tsp	oriental sesame oil (optional)	5 mL
1 tbsp	Dijon mustard	15 mL
2 tbsp	honey	25 mL

1. Cut the racks of ribs in half. Cook the ribs in simmering water for 30 minutes. Drain and cool.

2. Combine the remaining ingredients. Marinate the ribs for 1 hour or overnight.

3. Barbecue for 10 to 15 minutes per side (or bake for 10 to 15 minutes per side at 400°F/200°C). Brush with any excess marinade during the cooking.

Chinese-style Pork

Serves 4 to 6

This can be served as a main course, or cold as an appetizer. The sauce can also be used over chicken or turkey breasts. Five spice powder is actually a combination of six spices—fennel seed, anise, ginger, licorice root, cinnamon and cloves!

2 tbsp	Hoisin sauce	25 mL
1 tbsp	oyster sauce	15 mL
2 tbsp	soy sauce	25 mL
1 tbsp	rice wine	15 mL
1 tbsp	hot Chinese chili paste	15 mL
3 tbsp	honey	50 mL
1 tsp	salt	5 mL
¼ tsp	freshly ground pepper	1 mL
½ tsp	five spice powder (optional)	2 mL
2	cloves garlic, minced	2
1 tbsp	finely chopped ginger root	15 mL
2 lb	pork tenderloin or centre cut boneless pork loin, cut into pieces lengthwise, about 2 in/5 cm thick	1 kg

1. Combine all the ingredients except for the pork.
2. Place the pieces of pork and the marinade in a plastic bag and marinate for 2 to 4 hours at room temperature or overnight in the refrigerator.
3. Barbecue or roast at 350°F/180°C for 30 to 45 minutes, turning frequently. (If using a meat thermometer, the meat should register 160°F/70°C when done.)

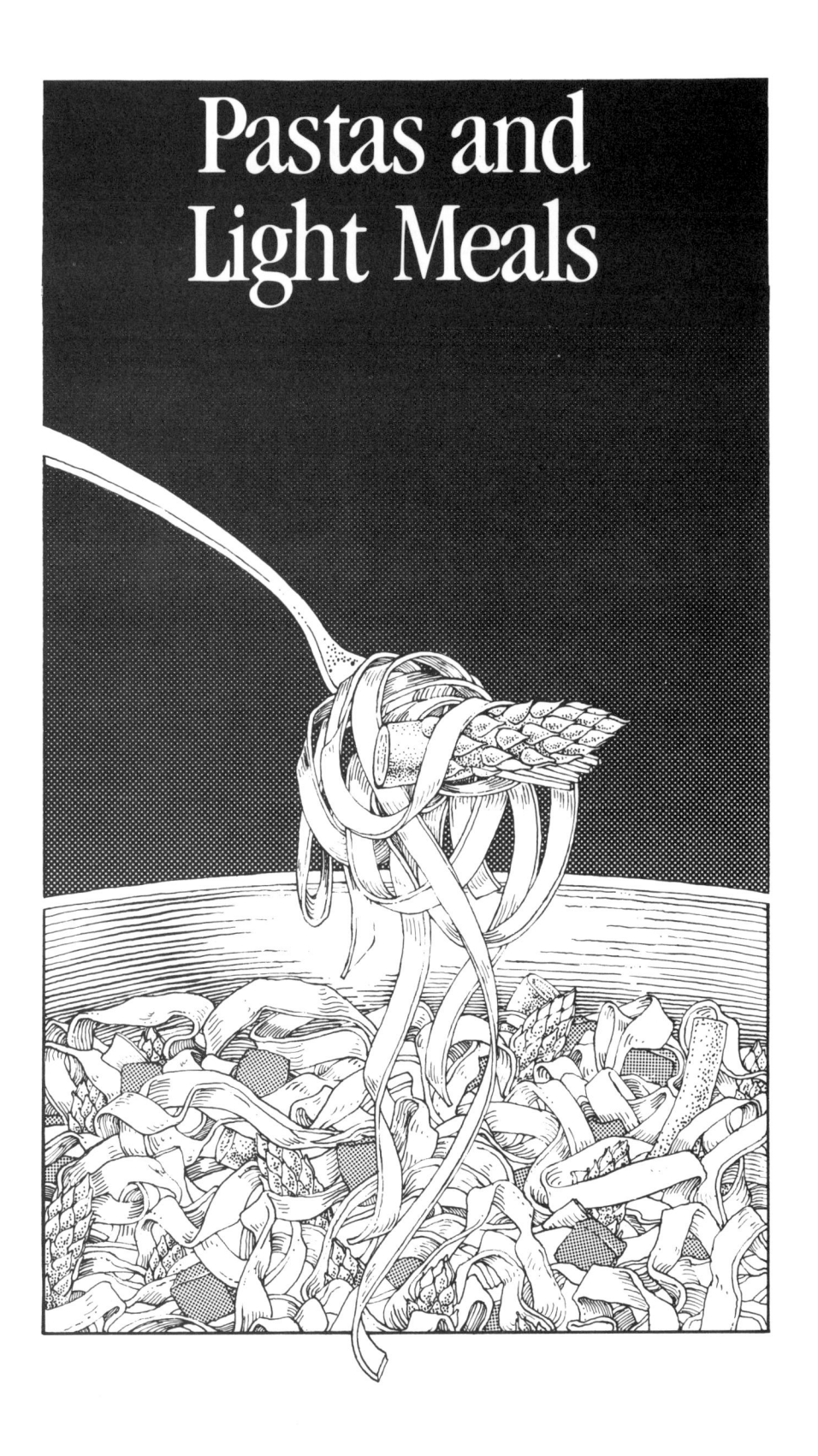

Pastas and Light Meals

Penne with Mixed Sausages and Red Peppers

Serves 6 to 8

This recipe was a result of a delicious trip to the St. Lawrence Market in Toronto. The array of homemade sausages was an inspiration.

Penne are the noodles that look like pen nibs, but you can use rigatoni instead. I served this to Jacques Pépin when he came to dinner, and although I tried to be nonchalant, I was a nervous wreck. I needn't have worried—he really loves down-to-earth home cooking.

2	hot Italian sausages (approx. 3 oz/100 g each)	2
2	sweet Italian sausages (approx. 3 oz/100 g each)	2
¼ cup	olive oil	50 mL
3	cloves garlic, minced	3
¼ tsp	hot red chili flakes	1 mL
1	red onion, chopped	1
8 oz	Polish sausage, sliced into ½-in/1-cm slices	250 g
3	red peppers, peeled and cut into 2-in/5-cm chunks	3
3	tomatoes, peeled, seeded and chopped	3
	Salt and freshly ground pepper to taste	
1 lb	penne noodles	500 g
2 tbsp	unsalted butter	25 mL
½ cup	grated Parmesan cheese (preferably Parmigiano Reggiano)	125 mL
2 tbsp	chopped fresh Italian parsley and/or basil	25 mL

1. Prick the Italian sausages in a few places and place in a deep skillet. Cover with cold water and bring to a boil. Reduce the heat and simmer gently for 30 minutes. Cool, peel off the casings and slice the sausages into pieces approximately 1 in/2.5 cm thick.

2. Heat the oil in deep skillet or Dutch oven and add the garlic, chili flakes and onion. Cook over medium heat until tender and fragrant but do not brown. Add the Polish sausage and red peppers and cook until the peppers wilt. Add the cooked hot and sweet Italian sausage slices and tomatoes. Cook for about 5 minutes.

3. Add a little salt and pepper. Cook, stirring occasionally, for about 20 minutes. Taste and adjust seasoning if necessary. (The dish can be made ahead up to this point.)

4. Just before serving, cook the penne in a large pot of boiling salted water until tender. Drain well and toss the pasta with the butter and sausage sauce. Sprinkle with cheese and parsley or basil. Toss well and serve immediately.

PASTAS AND LIGHT MEALS

Fettuccine with Smoked Chicken and Hazelnuts

Serves 4 to 6

Jack Kwinter of Toronto makes the best smoked chicken I have ever tasted. His smoked meats are lower in salt than most—even Mark loves them. If you cannot find smoked chicken, use smoked turkey or ham. For a lighter version, use a cup of tomato puree instead of the whipping cream.

2 tbsp	unsalted butter	25 mL
1 cup	whipping cream	250 mL
2 cups	diced smoked chicken meat	500 mL
	Salt and freshly ground pepper to taste	
8 oz	chèvre (unripened goat cheese)	250 g
½ cup	finely chopped toasted hazelnuts	125 mL
¼ cup	grated Parmesan cheese (preferably Parmigiano Reggiano)	50 mL
1 lb	fettuccine noodles	500 g
2 tbsp	chopped fresh parsley	25 mL

1. Melt the butter in a large skillet and add the cream. Bring to a boil.
2. Add the chicken and cook until the chicken is heated through. Season lightly with salt and pepper. Keep warm.
3. In a large bowl, break up the chèvre into small pieces. Sprinkle with the nuts and Parmesan cheese.
4. Just before serving, cook the fettuccine in a large pot of boiling salted water. Cook until tender but still slightly firm. Drain well.
5. Add the fettuccine to the cheese and nuts. Pour the hot chicken-cream mixture on top. Toss well. Taste and adjust seasoning if necessary. Sprinkle with parsley.

Linguine with Smoked Salmon and Lemon Sauce

Serves 6 as an appetizer

This is great as an appetizer. Or you can leave out the smoked salmon and serve it with a main course such as roast chicken or lamb. You could also substitute smoked ham for the salmon.

¼ cup	unsalted butter	50 mL
2	cloves garlic, finely chopped	2
1 cup	whipping cream	250 mL
	Peel of one lemon	
8 oz	smoked salmon, diced	250 g
2 tbsp	lemon juice	25 mL
1 tsp	salt	5 mL
1 lb	linguine	500 g
2 tbsp	vodka	25 mL
½ cup	grated Parmesan cheese (preferably Parmigiano Reggiano)	125 mL
	Salt, freshly ground pepper and nutmeg to taste	
2 tbsp	chopped fresh dill or green onions	25 mL

1. Heat the butter in a large skillet and cook the garlic until fragrant and tender but not brown. Add the cream and boil gently until slightly thickened, about 5 minutes. Add the smoked salmon and cook just until heated through.

2. Meanwhile, bring a large pot of water to a boil and add the salt. Add the linguine. If using dried pasta, cook for about 12 minutes until tender; cook fresh pasta for about 4 minutes.

3. Drain the linguine well and toss with the cream mixture, lemon juice, vodka and cheese. Toss until the cream clings to the pasta and thickens. Season with salt, pepper and nutmeg. Sprinkle with fresh dill.

PASTAS AND LIGHT MEALS

Oriental Pesto with Noodles
Serves 6 to 8

I first tasted this unusual version of pesto in San Francisco at the home of my friend Loni Kuhn. We met when we attended Marcella Hazan's classes in Italy and have been fast friends ever since. One of the nice things about taking cooking classes is the people you meet, not just what you learn. Loni is a fabulous cook and cooking teacher and has introduced me to many wonderful dishes, including this one.

Basically there are three different types of parsley—the regular curly-leaf parsley, the flat-leaf Italian parsley, and Chinese parsley, sometimes known as fresh coriander or cilantro. The first two types are similar, and can be used interchangeably. But Chinese parsley has quite a different taste altogether. It is usually available in Chinese markets (ask for Chinese parsley) or in West Indian and Mexican markets (cilantro) or East Indian markets (call it fresh coriander). It may seem to be hard to find, but you have to call it by its right name at the right store. If you really can't find it, just use more parsley.

½ cup	peanut oil	125 mL
1 cup	unsalted peanuts	250 mL
4	cloves garlic, peeled	4
1	1-in/2.5-cm piece ginger root, peeled	1
2	banana peppers, seeded and ribbed	2
¼ tsp	hot red chili flakes (optional)	1 mL
½ cup	packed fresh basil leaves	125 mL
½ cup	packed fresh mint leaves	125 mL
½ cup	packed fresh parsley	125 mL
½ cup	packed fresh Chinese parsley	125 mL
1 tsp	salt (or more to taste)	5 mL
¼ cup	lemon juice	50 mL
1 tbsp	salt	15 mL
1½ lb	fettuccine or linguine noodles	750 g

1. Heat the oil in a skillet and brown the peanuts carefully. Do not allow them to burn. Drain on paper towels and cool.

2. In a food processor fitted with the steel knife, chop the garlic and ginger into a paste. Add the peppers and chop. Add the nuts and chop.

3. Add the herbs and chop until very fine and the mixture is well blended.

4. Add 1 tsp/15 mL salt and the lemon juice and taste. Adjust seasonings if necessary. Reserve until ready to serve.

5. Bring a large pot of water to a boil. Add 1 tbsp/15 mL salt. Add the noodles and cook until tender. Stir about ¼ cup/50 mL of the boiling water into the pesto to warm it. Drain the pasta and shake out the excess water. Toss with the sauce and serve immediately.

Fettuccine with Ham and Asparagus

Serves 4 as an appetizer

In the spring when the first asparagus appears on the market, this makes a wonderful appetizer or Easter brunch dish. It is as beautiful as it is flavourful.

1 lb	fresh asparagus	500 g
⅓ cup	unsalted butter	75 mL
1	clove garlic, finely chopped	1
½ cup	chicken stock or water	125 mL
1 cup	whipping cream	250 mL
4 oz	cooked ham, diced	125 g
	Salt and freshly ground pepper to taste	
1 tsp	Russian-style mustard (such as Honeycup)	5 mL
pinch	cayenne pepper	pinch
1 lb	fettuccine	500 g
3 tbsp	chopped fresh dill	50 mL
1 cup	grated Parmesan cheese (preferably Parmigiano Reggiano)	250 mL

1. Cut the tips off the asparagus and cook gently in boiling water until tender, about 3 to 5 minutes. Drain well.

2. Trim off the tough bases of the asparagus and discard. Peel the stems only if they are tough. Dice.

3. Melt half the butter in a skillet and add the garlic and diced asparagus. Cook until fragrant.

4. Add the chicken stock and cook until reduced to a few tablespoons. Add the cream and ham and cook until the sauce has reduced slightly and thickened. Season lightly with salt and pepper and stir in the mustard and cayenne.

5. Bring a large pot of salted water to a boil. When the sauce is ready, add the pasta to the water and cook until tender. If the pasta has been freshly made, it should take only a minute. Store-bought "fresh" pasta usually takes 5 to 6 minutes and commercial dried pasta usually takes 10 to 12 minutes.

6. Drain the pasta well and place it in a large flat bowl. Add the remaining butter, dill and cheese. Pour over the sauce and toss well. Taste and adjust seasoning if necessary.

PASTAS AND LIGHT MEALS

Spaghetti with Seafood Sauce *Serves 4 to 6*

The inspiration for this recipe came after taking Marcella Hazan's cooking course in Bologna. Her recipes were so outstanding that I invited her to teach at my school. She's a very serious, intense teacher, and is always very popular with students who feel that they've come to the oracle of Italian cooking when they attend her classes.

⅓ cup	olive oil (or more if necessary)	75 mL
3	cloves garlic, finely chopped	3
¼ tsp	hot red chili flakes	1 mL
¼ cup	chopped fresh parsley or basil	50 mL
8 oz	scallops, chopped	250 g
8 oz	shrimp, shelled, deveined and chopped	250 g
1 lb	spaghetti	500 g
⅓ cup	toasted fresh breadcrumbs	75 mL
	Salt and freshly ground pepper	

1. Heat the oil in a large skillet. Cook the garlic and chili flakes and cook until fragrant but do not brown.

2. Add half the parsley and seafood. Cook for 2 to 3 minutes. Remove from heat.

3. Cook the spaghetti in a large pot of boiling salted water until tender. Drain well and toss with the sauce, breadcrumbs and remaining parsley. Season with salt and pepper to taste and serve immediately.

Penne with Creamy Sausage Sauce

Serves 6 to 8

I remember having a dish similar to this at a restaurant in Bologna. I dreamed about it for five years but for some reason never thought to make it. One night when I was having dinner at one of my favourite Italian restaurants, Mastro's, the owners, Rina and Livio Camaro, served me something very close to it. So I went back to my kitchen, and came up with this. For a tomato version, use one 28-oz/796-mL tin tomatoes, pureed, instead of the cream. The sauce will be different but will have far fewer calories.

3 tbsp	extra-virgin olive oil	50 mL
3	cloves garlic, minced	3
¼ tsp	hot red chili flakes (optional)	1 mL
1 lb	sweet Italian sausages, removed from casings and crumbled	500 g
1 cup	whipping cream	250 mL
1 tsp	salt	5 mL
¼ tsp	freshly ground pepper	1 mL
¼ tsp	nutmeg	1 mL
1 lb	penne	500 g
3 tbsp	unsalted butter	50 mL
½ cup	grated Parmesan cheese (preferably Parmigiano Reggiano)	125 mL
2 tbsp	chopped fresh parsley or basil	25 mL

1 Heat the oil in a large skillet. Add the garlic, hot red chili flakes and crumbled sausage meat. Cook until all traces of pink disappear, about 5 minutes.

2 Add the whipping cream, salt, pepper and nutmeg and bring to a boil. Reduce the heat and simmer gently for about 10 minutes or until the cream reduces and sauce thickens somewhat.

3 Meanwhile, cook the pasta in a large pot of boiling, salted water. Drain the noodles well but do not rinse.

4 Toss the noodles with the sauce, butter, cheese and parsley. Taste and adjust seasonings if necessary.

Spaghetti alla Carbonara

Serves 4

Although there are so many recipes for this famous dish, this is my favourite. Carbonara refers to the freshly ground black pepper that is sprinkled on top of this dish just before serving. It is said to resemble coal dust, which is where the word carbonara comes from.

4 oz	bacon, diced	125 g
2	cloves garlic, chopped	2
3 tbsp	olive oil	50 mL
½ tsp	hot red chili flakes (or less to taste)	2 mL
2	eggs	2
⅓ cup	grated Parmesan cheese (preferably Parmigiano Reggiano)	75 mL
1 lb	spaghetti	500 g
	Salt and freshly ground pepper to taste	

1. Place the bacon and chopped garlic in a large skillet with the olive oil. Add the hot peppers. Cook on low heat for 12 to 15 minutes until all the fat is rendered and the bacon is browned.
2. Beat the eggs in a bowl with the cheese.
3. Cook the spaghetti in boiling salted water for about 12 minutes. Drain and place in a serving bowl. Quickly spoon over the bacon mixture. Toss. Quickly stir in the eggs and cheese. Add some salt, lots of pepper and toss well. Serve immediately.

Bugialli's Fresh Tomato Sauce with Spaghetti

Serves 4 to 6

It is hard to believe something this good could be so easy. It's one of my favourite recipes from Giuliano Bugialli, popular Italian cooking teacher. Giuliano comes to Toronto every year and delights my students with tales of Italian history, music and literature. He's a true Renaissance man.

2 lb	ripe tomatoes	1 kg
½ cup	olive oil	125 mL
1	50-g tin anchovy fillets, minced	1
2	cloves garlic, minced	2
¼ tsp	hot red chili flakes (or more to taste)	1 mL
	Salt and freshly ground pepper to taste	
1 lb	spaghetti	500 g
	Chopped fresh parsley	

1. Preheat the oven to 400°F/200°C.
2. Slice the tomatoes and arrange in large baking dish. (It doesn't matter if the tomatoes are layered.) Add the olive oil and sprinkle with anchovies, garlic, chili flakes, salt and pepper.
3. Bake for 30 to 40 minutes or until the tomatoes are tender and break up when touched with a wooden spoon.
4. Cook the spaghetti for 10 to 12 minutes. Drain well (do not rinse) and add to the tomatoes. Toss gently. To serve, sprinkle with parsley.

PASTAS AND
LIGHT MEALS

Macaroni and Cheese

Serves 6 to 8

You just can't beat good macaroni and cheese. The unusual twist to this version is curry powder—it does not dominate, but rather adds a subtle, mysterious flavour.

	8 oz	macaroni noodles	250 g
	¼ cup	unsalted butter	50 mL
	⅓ cup	all-purpose flour	75 mL
	3 cups	milk, hot	750 mL
	1 tbsp	Dijon mustard	15 mL
	1 tsp	curry powder	5 mL
	1 tsp	salt	5 mL
	¼ tsp	freshly ground pepper	1 mL
	1 tsp	Worcestershire sauce	5 mL
	¼ tsp	Tabasco sauce	1 mL
	¼ tsp	nutmeg	1 mL
	2 cups	grated Cheddar cheese	500 mL
TOPPING	1 cup	fresh breadcrumbs	250 mL
	½ cup	grated Cheddar cheese	125 mL
	¼ cup	unsalted butter, melted	50 mL

1 Preheat the oven to 350°F/180°C.

2 Bring a large pot of salted water to a boil. Cook the macaroni until tender; do not overcook. Drain in a colander and rinse with cold water. Reserve.

3 While the macaroni is cooking, prepare the sauce. Melt ¼ cup/50 mL butter in a saucepan and add the flour. Cook on low heat and stir for about 5 minutes.

4 Whisk in the hot milk and bring to a boil. Reduce the heat and add seasonings.

5 Add 2 cups/500 mL cheese and cook gently for 5 minutes more, or until the cheese melts. Taste again and adjust seasonings.

6 Combine the sauce with the macaroni and place in a buttered 9-in x 13-in/3-L casserole dish.

7 Combine all the topping ingredients and spread over the top. Bake for 30 minutes or until the sauce bubbles and the top browns.

Fettuccine California Style

Serves 6 to 8

Chèvre or goat cheese has always been popular in Europe. But it wasn't until they started making excellent goat cheese in California, and California chefs and food writers started to promote it, that it became so popular all across North America.

This creamy, luscious sauce works well with white or green pasta. I like to use a mild, creamy-style Canadian goat cheese.

¼ cup	unsalted butter	50 mL
1	clove garlic, minced	1
1½ cups	whipping cream	375 mL
6 oz	unripened, soft goat cheese	175 mL
1 tsp	chopped fresh rosemary (or ¼ tsp/1 mL dried)	5 mL
1 tsp	chopped fresh thyme (or ¼ tsp/1 mL dried)	5 mL
1 tbsp	chopped fresh basil or parsley	15 mL
1 tsp	salt	5 mL
½ tsp	freshly ground pepper	2 mL
1 lb	white or green fettuccine noodles	500 g
¼ cup	grated Parmesan cheese (preferably Parmigiano Reggiano)	50 mL

1. To make the sauce, melt half the butter in a skillet. Add the garlic and cook gently, without browning, until fragrant. Add the cream and bring to a boil. Cook until the liquid reduces and thickens slightly.
2. Whisk the goat cheese into the cream until smooth. Add the herbs, salt and pepper.
3. Cook the pasta in a large pot of boiling salted water until tender. Drain well. Toss with the sauce, Parmesan cheese and remaining butter. Taste and adjust seasonings if necessary.

PASTAS AND LIGHT MEALS

Spaghettini with Sun-dried Tomatoes

Serves 6 to 8

This is great to serve as a light meal or as an appetizer. All kinds of wonderful ingredients like wild mushrooms, sun-dried tomatoes and fresh herbs make this dish spectacular.

Spaghettini is thinner spaghetti. Of course, if you can't find it, use spaghetti instead.

1 oz	dried wild mushrooms (approx.)	30 g
¾ cup	warm water	175 mL
½ cup	extra-virgin olive oil	125 mL
3	cloves garlic, finely chopped	3
¼ tsp	hot red chili flakes	1 mL
¼ cup	sun-dried tomatoes, cut into strips	50 mL
4 oz	fresh mushrooms, sliced	125 g
½ cup	black olives, pitted and cut into large pieces (preferably Kalamata)	125 mL
1 tsp	salt	5 mL
¼ tsp	freshly ground pepper	1 mL
1 lb	spaghettini	500 g
¼ cup	chopped fresh basil or parsley	50 mL

1. Place the dried mushrooms in the warm water and allow them to soak for 30 minutes. Drain the mushrooms, reserving the liquid. Wash the mushrooms to get rid of any sand or dirt and cut them into strips. Reserve. Strain the soaking liquid through a coffee filter or paper towels and reserve.
2. Heat half of the olive oil in a large skillet and add the garlic and chili flakes. Cook, without browning, until very fragrant.
3. Add the tomatoes, fresh mushrooms, dried mushrooms and the soaking liquid. Cook until the liquid in the pan has almost evaporated.
4. Add the olives, salt and pepper. Remove from the heat.
5. Cook the pasta in a large pot of boiling, salted water. Drain well. Reheat the sauce just before the pasta is ready. Toss the pasta with the sauce, basil and remaining olive oil. Taste and adjust seasonings if necessary.

Spaghetti with Pesto Sauce

Serves 8 to 10 as an appetizer

This is an all-time favourite summer recipe. The sauce can also be frozen, for a fresh taste of basil all year round, and keeps for about two weeks in the refrigerator. It can also be stirred into rice or mashed potatoes or can be used as a pizza topping. And it is wonderful served as a condiment with lamb.

3	cloves garlic, peeled	3
½ cup	pine nuts	125 mL
1 cup	packed fresh parsley leaves	250 mL
2 cups	packed fresh basil leaves	500 mL
1 cup	grated Parmesan cheese (preferably Parmigiano Reggiano)	250 mL
½ cup	extra-virgin olive oil	125 mL
1 tsp	salt	5 mL
¼ tsp	freshly ground pepper	1 mL
1½ lb	spaghetti	750 g
¼ cup	unsalted butter	50 mL

1. Place the garlic in a food processor or blender and process until finely chopped. Add the nuts and chop until very fine. (If you are not using a blender or food processor, chop finely with a knife or use a mortar and pestle.)
2. Chop the parsley and basil and add to the garlic-nut mixture. Blend in the cheese.
3. Slowly beat in the olive oil—the mixture should be thick. Season with salt and pepper. (The dish can be made ahead to this point.)
4. Cook the spaghetti in a large pot of boiling salted water.
5. Just before the spaghetti is ready, add ¼ cup/50 mL boiling spaghetti water to the pesto sauce to warm it gently. Drain the spaghetti and toss with the butter and sauce.

PASTAS AND
LIGHT MEALS

Cheese Tart with Yeast Pastry

Serves 8 to 10

The idea for this tart came from a lunch I enjoyed at La Varenne, one of Paris's top cooking schools. I attended the school in 1976 after it first opened. If you are interested in cooking and are visiting Paris, the school often offers afternoon demonstration classes which are open to the public.

YEAST CRUST			
2 cups	all-purpose flour	500 mL	
1	envelope yeast	1	
½ cup	warm milk	125 mL	
2	eggs	2	
1 tsp	salt	5 mL	
⅓ cup	unsalted butter, at room temperature	75 mL	
FILLING			
6 oz	diced ham	175 g	
6 oz	Swiss cheese, grated	175 g	
2	eggs	2	
2	egg yolks	2	
1 cup	whipping cream or crème fraîche	250 mL	
	Salt and freshly ground pepper to taste		
pinch	nutmeg	pinch	
2 tbsp	unsalted butter, cut into bits	25 mL	

1 Sift the flour into a bowl and make a well in the centre. Add the yeast. Pour half the milk over the yeast and allow it to dissolve, about 5 minutes.

2 Pour in the rest of the milk, 2 eggs and 1 tsp/5 mL salt. Gather the dough together with your fingers. (The dough will be very moist and sticky.) Knead the dough for about 5 minutes by slapping it against the sides of the bowl. Beat in ⅓ cup/75 mL butter. (The dough may still be sticky.)

3 Place the dough in an oiled bowl, cover and allow to rise in a warm place for 1 to 1½ hours or until doubled in bulk.

4 When the dough has risen, punch it down and place in a 10-in/25-cm springform pan. Flatten the dough with your hands and push it up the sides of the pan to line it. Do not worry if the dough doesn't stay perfectly where you press it.

5 Arrange the ham and cheese over the bottom of the dough. Beat 2 eggs with the egg yolks, cream, salt, pepper and nutmeg. Pour over the ham and cheese. Dot with 2 tbsp/25 mL butter. Allow to rest for 15 minutes before baking.

6 Preheat the oven to 400°F/200°C. Bake for 1 hour or until the filling is brown and the pastry is crisp. Serve hot, warm or cold.

Caramelized Apple Pancakes

Serves 3 to 4

My husband, who loves apples, loves me more when I make this for him. This makes two or three 8-in/20-cm pancakes. Some people like to eat a whole one, but half is usually enough. Serve with maple syrup. (The batter, without the caramelized apples, makes wonderful pancakes on its own.)

2	medium-sized apples	2
½ cup	sugar	125 mL
2 tbsp	unsalted butter	25 mL
2	eggs	2
1½ cups	buttermilk	375 mL
1 cup	all-purpose flour	250 mL
¾ tsp	baking soda	4 mL
¼ tsp	salt	1 mL
2 tbsp	sugar	25 mL
¼ cup	unsalted butter	50 mL

1. Peel the apples and cut them in half. Core and slice thinly.

2. Place ½ cup/125 mL sugar in a heavy skillet and heat until it begins to turn a caramel colour. Do not stir. Add 2 tbsp/25 mL butter. Stir until melted. Do not worry if the mixture is lumpy.

3. Add the apples and cook them until tender, about 10 minutes. Stir occasionally. Reserve.

4. Prepare the pancake batter by beating the eggs with the buttermilk. Sift or mix together the flour, baking soda, salt and 2 tbsp/25 mL sugar. Stir into the egg mixture.

5. Melt ¼ cup/50 mL butter in an 8-in/20-cm omelette pan, crêpe pan or non-stick pan. Stir the melted butter into the batter.

6. Place about ½ cup/125 mL batter in the hot pan. Cook a little and then arrange some of the apples on top. Pour more batter on to cover the apples—about another ½ cup/125 mL. Cook for a few minutes.

7. Flip by slipping the pancake out of the pan onto a plate and then flipping it back into pan to cook the other side. Cook for another few minutes.

8. Repeat with the remaining batter and apples. If you have extra apples, serve them over the pancakes.

PASTAS AND
LIGHT MEALS

Passover Bubelechs (Pancakes) *Serves 3 to 4*

My mother always makes these pancakes at Passover for breakfast or lunch. They are my father's favourite treat. This is my mum's recipe and it is the best! Serve the bubelechs with sugar or jam.

3	eggs, separated	3
¼ cup	water	50 mL
⅔ cup	matzah meal	150 mL
2 tbsp	vegetable oil	25 mL

1. Beat the egg yolks lightly with the water.
2. Beat the egg whites until light. Fold into the egg yolk-water mixture. Fold in the matzah meal.
3. Heat the oil in a large skillet and drop the batter into the hot pan in large spoonfuls. Flatten the pancakes slightly. You may have to cook the pancakes in two batches. Cook for a few minutes on each side until nicely browned and cooked through.

Vegetables

Swiss Chard Italian Style

Serves 6

Swiss chard is an unusual vegetable, because you can use both the tender green leaves and the tougher stalks. I like to cook the two parts separately because of their very different nature. These two dishes can be served at the same meal or separately. Instead of the Swiss chard stalks, fennel, celery or leeks could be used. Instead of the Swiss chard greens, spinach could be used.

2 lb	Swiss chard	1 kg
	Salt and freshly ground pepper to taste	
¼ cup	unsalted butter	50 mL
¼ cup	grated Parmesan cheese (preferably Parmigiano Reggiano)	50 mL
2	cloves garlic, minced	2

1. Preheat the oven to 350°F/180°C.
2. Cut the leaves of Swiss chard from the stalks (see below). Break the leaves up into pieces and wash and dry them well. Reserve.
3. Cut the stalks into 2-in/5-cm pieces. Wash them well. Cook in boiling water to cover for 10 minutes or until tender. Drain well.
4. Place the stalks in a buttered gratin dish and sprinkle with salt and pepper. Dot with half the butter and the cheese. Bake for 30 minutes and serve.
5. To prepare the leaves, melt the remaining butter in a large skillet. Cook the garlic until tender and fragrant but do not brown. Add the leaves and cook for about 6 minutes until wilted and tender. Sprinkle with salt and pepper and serve.

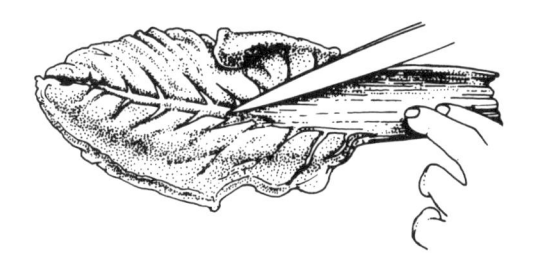

Glazed Zucchini with Sesame

Serves 4 to 6

This is a recipe from Japanese cooking expert Elizabeth Andoh. Every year Elizabeth comes to Toronto to teach at my school, where students are always so excited to learn more about Japanese ingredients, techniques and, most of all, culture. Elizabeth has two excellent cookbooks, At Home with Japanese Cooking *(Knopf, 1980) and* An American Taste of Japan *(Morrow, 1985). This recipe is very easy and can add an oriental flavour to any meal.*

1 tbsp	sesame seeds	15 mL
1¼ lb	slender zucchini (about 4 medium)	625 g
2 tbsp	vegetable oil	25 mL
1 tbsp	Japanese rice wine (sake)	15 mL
4 tsp	soy sauce	20 mL
½ tsp	sugar	2 mL

1. In a clean, dry skillet, roast the sesame seeds over medium-high heat for approximately 30 seconds or until a few pop and colour slightly. Set aside 1 tsp/5 mL whole seeds. Mince the remaining seeds as you would parsley. Reserve.

2. Wash and dry the zucchini. Cut off the stem ends. Using a circular motion, rub the cut surface with this stump. A white foam will appear. The Japanese refer to this as *aku* or bitterness, and they prefer to remove this from vine vegetables before cooking them. Rinse away the foam and pat dry again. Cut off and discard the opposite ends. Cut the zucchini into quarters lengthwise, and cut the strips into approximately 1½-in/4-cm pieces.

3. Heat the oil in a large skillet and add the zucchini. Cook over high heat for 2 minutes, stirring constantly.

4. Add the wine, cook for a few seconds and then add the soy sauce and sugar. Simmer, covered, for 1 minute. Remove the lid, sprinkle the zucchini with the minced sesame seeds and cook over high heat, stirring constantly, for another 15 to 20 seconds or until the zucchini appears glazed and any liquid has evaporated.

5. Sprinkle with the reserved whole sesame seeds before serving. Serve hot or at room temperature.

Asparagus Marco Polo

Serves 4 to 6

This recipe is adapted from one presented by James Barber, Vancouver cooking school owner and cookbook author, at the 1986 March of Dimes Celebrity Gourmet Gala. It is one of the best ways I have ever had asparagus, and is also delicious served cold.

When James Barber explained how to cut the asparagus for this recipe, he said to place the asparagus in line with 12 o'clock and 6 o'clock and to cut it at an 11 o'clock angle. I found it easier to place the asparagus in line with 9 o'clock and 3 o'clock and to cut at a 10 o'clock angle (if you're left-handed it's probably completely different!). These instructions sounded very crazy on the radio (and they don't sound much better here!), but in the end it doesn't really matter.

1½ lb	asparagus	750 g
3 tbsp	corn or safflower oil	50 mL
2 tbsp	fresh ginger root, cut into tiny matchstick pieces	25 mL
½ tsp	salt	2 mL
1 tsp	sugar	5 mL
2 tbsp	lemon juice	25 mL

1. Cut off the tough stems of the asparagus. If you wish, peel the stems partway up with a vegetable peeler.
2. Cut the asparagus into pieces about ½ in/1 cm thick, on a sharp diagonal (see below).
3. Heat the oil in a skillet. Add the ginger and cook for a few seconds until fragrant.
4. Add the asparagus, sprinkle with the salt and toss with the oil. Cook for 1 or 2 minutes. Add the sugar, toss, cover and cook for 2 or 3 minutes.
5. Add the lemon juice. Toss well and serve.

Spinach with Raisins and Pine Nuts

Serves 4

This unusual combination of flavours with spinach is quite common in Spain and Italy, but not often found here. Try it—it's great.

1½ lb	spinach	750 g
½ cup	raisins	125 mL
1 cup	boiling water	250 mL
⅓ cup	pine nuts	75 mL
2 tbsp	olive oil	25 mL
2	cloves garlic, minced	2
4	anchovy fillets, minced	4
	Salt and freshly ground pepper to taste	

1. Preheat the oven to 350°F/180°C.
2. Remove and discard the tough stems from the spinach. Wash the spinach well and place it in a large pot with just the water from the washing clinging to the leaves. Cover and cook just until wilted. Cool and gently squeeze out the excess water with your hands. Chop coarsely.
3. Meanwhile, place the raisins in a bowl, cover with the boiling water and soak for 10 minutes. Drain.
4. Place the pine nuts on a cookie sheet and bake for 3 to 5 minutes or until lightly browned.
5. Just before serving, heat the oil in a skillet and add the garlic and anchovies. Cook on medium heat until fragrant, but do not brown. Add the raisins and spinach and toss well until the spinach is thoroughly heated. Season with salt and pepper if necessary (anchovies are very salty). Sprinkle with the toasted pine nuts.

Mixed Red, Yellow and Green Peppers

Serves 6 to 8

This recipe can be served as an appetizer, salad, sauce or vegetable. You can serve it as an appetizer or salad with a little red wine vinegar, garlic, capers, chopped anchovies and olive oil. (If you are serving it as a salad or appetizer, simply char and peel the peppers and combine with the above ingredients. They do not need further cooking.) You can also serve this as a topping for pasta or on veal or chicken. As a vegetable, it goes beautifully with any plainly cooked roast or chop.

If you cannot find red, yellow and green peppers, just use more of the colours you can find.

4	**red peppers**	4
4	**green peppers**	4
4	**yellow peppers**	4
¼ cup	**olive oil**	50 mL
3	**cloves garlic, minced**	3
¼ tsp	**hot red chili flakes**	1 mL
½ tsp	**salt**	2 mL
½ tsp	**freshly ground pepper**	2 mL
¼ cup	**chopped fresh basil or parsley**	50 mL

1. Place the peppers on a baking sheet and broil until black and charred. Turn the peppers over and char other side. Repeat until they are charred all over. (Instead of broiling the peppers, they can be barbecued.)

2. Cool the peppers and peel off the blackened skin. (Some people put the peppers in a paper or plastic bag to cool—they feel the skins come off more easily—but I find it makes little difference.) Underneath the pepper should be colourful with only touches of dark spots.

3. Halve the peppers and discard the ribs and seeds. Cut into large pieces.

4. Heat the oil in large skillet and add the garlic and hot pepper flakes. Add the peppers and cook for 10 to 15 minutes. Season with salt, pepper and basil.

Cheese-baked Vegetable Custard

Serves 6 to 8

This recipe is roughly based on one taught at Lydie Marshall's wonderful cooking school in New York City. She has a large, warm, French-Provincial kitchen in the basement of her brownstone that welcomes students with its friendly, delicious aromas. This delicious custard is full of vegetables and cheese.

2 tbsp	unsalted butter	25 mL
8 oz	bacon, thickly sliced and diced	250 g
2	onions, chopped	2
2	cloves garlic, minced	2
2	leeks, white part only, sliced	2
1 lb	cabbage, chopped, cooked and drained	500 g
2 lb	spinach, washed, cooked, squeezed dry and coarsely chopped	1 kg
4	eggs	4
1 cup	whipping cream	250 mL
1½ tsp	salt	7 mL
¼ tsp	freshly ground pepper	1 mL
1 cup	grated Swiss cheese (approx. 4 oz/125 g)	250 mL
¼ cup	grated Parmesan cheese (preferably Parmigiano Reggiano)	50 mL

1. Preheat the oven to 375°F/190°C.
2. Heat the butter in a skillet and cook the bacon until crisp. Drain the bacon but do not discard the fat.
3. Cook the onions, garlic and leeks in the bacon fat until tender. Stir in the cabbage and spinach.
4. In a large bowl, beat the eggs with the cream, salt and pepper. Add the vegetables, reserved bacon bits and Swiss cheese.
5. Transfer the mixture to a buttered 3-qt/3-L shallow casserole dish and sprinkle with Parmesan. Bake for 1 hour.

Curried Pureed Parsnips

Serves 6 to 8

When this recipe was aired on the radio, I told everyone that I felt sorry for parsnips, and that even though this was one of the most delicious vegetable dishes I had ever tasted, I didn't think anyone would write in for the recipe. To our surprise and delight, lots of people asked for the recipe, saying that they liked parsnips or were looking for a recipe to try them. We even received thank-you notes from people who tried this and loved it!

This recipe can also be made with carrots, turnips or sweet potatoes, or a combination of pureed vegetables.

2 lb	parsnips, cleaned and sliced	1 kg
3 tbsp	unsalted butter	50 mL
2	cloves garlic, minced	2
2 tsp	curry powder	10 mL
½ tsp	cinnamon	2 mL
pinch	nutmeg	pinch
1 tsp	salt	5 mL
¼ tsp	freshly ground pepper	1 mL
½ cup	whipping cream	125 mL

1. Steam or boil the parsnips until they are tender, about 15 minutes. Drain them well.
2. Melt the butter in a small saucepan and add the garlic. Cook for a few minutes over medium-low heat until very fragrant and tender. Do not brown. Add the curry powder, cinnamon and nutmeg. Cook for a few minutes to release the flavours. Do not allow the mixture to burn.
3. Add the salt, pepper and cream to the mixture and heat well.
4. Puree or mash the cooked parsnips with the cream mixture until smooth. Taste and adjust the seasonings if necessary. Serve immediately or pipe or spread into a baking dish, cover with buttered parchment paper and reheat at 375°F/190°C for 20 to 25 minutes.

Candied Sweet Potatoes

Serves 6

This Southern-style sweet potato dish is great with any plain roast or meat dish. The potatoes can be served mashed or plain (if I overcook the potatoes by accident, I mash them!).

2 lb	sweet potatoes	1 kg
¼ cup	unsalted butter	50 mL
¼ cup	brown sugar	50 mL
¼ cup	orange juice	50 mL
½ tsp	salt	2 mL
½ tsp	cinnamon	2 mL
½ tsp	ginger	2 mL
pinch	allspice	pinch
pinch	nutmeg	pinch

1 Peel the sweet potatoes and cut them in half. Cover with boiling water and cook for 10 to 15 minutes or until about two-thirds cooked.

2 In a wide saucepan, melt the butter and add the remaining ingredients.

3 Cut the sweet potatoes into 2-in/5-cm cubes and add to the butter mixture. Combine well.

4 Cook over medium heat for 10 to 15 minutes or until liquid evaporates and the potatoes are cooked thoroughly and glazed. Serve as is or mash and spread in a casserole dish.

Bulgur Wheat Pilaf

Serves 4 to 6

If you have become tired of the vegetable dishes you have been serving lately, try this delicious alternative to rice. Bulgur is a staple in the Middle East and is actually cracked wheat that has been steamed and dried. If you have trouble finding it in the cereal section of a supermarket, try bulk food stores, health food stores or Middle Eastern specialty shops. It comes in three sizes of grains—for this recipe you'll need medium or large.

3 tbsp	**unsalted butter**	50 mL
1	**large red onion, diced**	1
1	**clove garlic, minced**	1
1½ cups	**medium- or large-grain bulgur wheat**	375 mL
3 cups	**chicken stock**	750 mL
	Salt and freshly ground pepper to taste	
3 tbsp	**chopped fresh parsley**	50 mL
3 tbsp	**chopped fresh dill**	50 mL

1 Melt the butter in a large saucepan. Add the onions and garlic and cook until tender and fragrant but do not brown.

2 Add the bulgur and combine well with the onion mixture, coating the grains well with the butter.

3 Add the stock, bring to a boil and then reduce the heat to low. Cover and simmer gently for 15 to 20 minutes or until all the liquid is absorbed.

4 Add some salt and pepper, the parsley and dill. Stir together gently. Taste and adjust seasonings if necessary.

Barbecued Potatoes and Onions

Serves 3 to 4

This is the perfect addition to any barbecue. I usually barbecue the potatoes before cooking the meat or fish and then keep them warm on the barbecue or in the oven while I'm preparing the rest of the meal. You can also use regular potatoes and regular cooking onions. It will be delicious anyway. The onions almost burn (sometimes they do!) and caramelize. The potatoes are tender and sweet from the onions.

You can add different things to this—basil, dill, parsley, cream, sour cream or yogurt. Just make up your own version. Peter Gzowski, the host of "Morningside" (where I'm an occasional guest), says this is one of his favourite recipes.

2 lb	baking potatoes	1 kg
2	red onions, sliced	2
	Salt and freshly ground pepper to taste	
½ tsp	rosemary	2 mL
¼ cup	unsalted butter, cut into bits	50 mL

1 Peel the potatoes and slice them ½ in/1 cm thick.

2 Butter the middle of a 24-in/60-cm piece of heavy-duty aluminum foil.

3 Arrange a layer of potatoes on the buttered section of foil. Top with a layer of onions. Season with salt, pepper and ¼ tsp/1 mL rosemary and dot with half the butter. Top with the remaining potatoes, onions, seasonings and butter. (Don't have more than two layers of potatoes, or they won't brown.)

4 Close the package tightly. Barbecue or grill for about 20 minutes. Turn the package and cook for 20 minutes longer.

Mashed Potatoes with Wild Mushrooms

Serves 4 to 6

Mashed potatoes are making a big comeback, but with style. Flavour plain mashed potatoes with a few spoonfuls of pesto sauce (see page 73) or olivada (see page 20), or make these wonderful mashed potatoes with wild mushrooms.

2 lb	baking potatoes	1 kg
1	1-oz/15-g package wild mushrooms	1
1 cup	boiling water	250 mL
2 tbsp	unsalted butter	25 mL
1	onion, diced	1
1	clove garlic, minced	1
8 oz	fresh mushrooms, sliced	250 g
¾ cup	whipping cream	175 mL
	Salt and freshly ground pepper to taste	
½ cup	grated Parmesan cheese (preferably Parmigiano Reggiano)	125 mL

1 Peel the potatoes and cut them into 2-in/5-cm pieces. Cover with cold water, bring to a boil and simmer until tender, about 20 minutes.

2 Meanwhile, place the dried wild mushrooms in a bowl and cover with the boiling water. Allow to soak for 20 minutes. Strain the soaking liquid through a paper towel-lined sieve to remove any sand or grit. Reserve the liquid. Rinse the mushrooms and chop. Reserve.

3 Melt the butter in a large skillet and add the onions and garlic. Cook until browned.

4 Add the fresh and wild mushrooms and cook until any liquid released from mushrooms evaporates. Add the soaking liquid from the mushrooms and cook until the liquid is absorbed by the mushrooms.

5 Add the cream and bring to a boil.

6 When the potatoes are tender, drain and pat dry. Mash or rice them. Beat in the mushroom mixture. Season to taste with salt and pepper and add the cheese. Serve immediately or spoon into a buttered casserole dish. Brush the top with a little melted butter and reheat at 350°F/180°C for 20 minutes just before serving.

Potato Latkes (Potato Pancakes)

Makes 16 3-in/7.5-cm pancakes

Every year at Chanukah, I usually air a recipe for potato latkes, or another Chanukah specialty. Potato latkes or pancakes are one of the most delicious of all Jewish festival foods. They're so delicious, in fact, that they are finally in vogue. I've seen many restaurants in California and New York serve mini potato pancakes, topped with sour cream and caviar, as an appetizer.

Potato pancakes should be served as soon as they are cooked, with sour cream or applesauce. They can be served as an appetizer, main course or side dish.

2	eggs	2
1	small onion, finely chopped or grated	1
3	large baking potatoes, peeled	3
1 tsp	salt	5 mL
¼ tsp	freshly ground pepper	1 mL
3 tbsp	matzah meal or cornflake crumbs	50 mL
	Oil for frying	

1. Combine the eggs with the grated onions.
2. Grate the potatoes into the egg mixture and stir well to prevent discoloration. (If you are doing this in a food processor, simply chop the onion with the steel knife, blend in the eggs and add the potatoes in chunks. Process until the potatoes are finely chopped.)
3. Add the salt, pepper and matzah meal.
4. Heat enough oil in a large skillet to measure ¾ in/2 cm deep. Add the batter to the oil by the spoonful and flatten each pancake with the back of the spoon. Cook until crisp, then turn and cook the second side.
5. Drain the pancakes as they are ready on paper towels. (When you cook each batch, add more oil if necessary, but add the oil in between the batches, and not while the pancakes are cooking.)

Salads and Salad Dressings

Marinated Vegetable Salad with Balsamic Vinegar Dressing

Serves 8 to 10

Balsamic vinegar is a sweet-tasting vinegar made by aging wine vinegar in four different kinds of wood—oak, chestnut, mulberry and juniper. When I visited the Fini factory outside Milan, we were taken into the vinegar "caves" and allowed to taste Balsamic vinegar that was 150 years old. You can sometimes buy these aged vinegars in specialty food shops for exorbitant prices, and Balsamic vinegar tastings have become as elitist as some wine tastings. However, even the "ordinary" Balsamic vinegar can be quite delicious—as long as you're not tasting it next to the 150-year-old variety!

Not only is this salad delicious, but it is really beautiful to look at. After the vegetables are cooked, plunge them into cold water to "set" the colour and texture. If you prefer a less-organized salad, simply toss all the vegetables with the dressing. It looks gorgeous this way, too.

1	small head cauliflower	1
1	small bunch broccoli	1
1 lb	asparagus or green beans	500 g
1 lb	carrots	500 g
2	tomatoes	2
1	bulb fresh fennel, trimmed and sliced	1
1 cup	black olives (preferably Kalamata)	250 mL
¼ cup	chopped fresh basil or parsley	50 mL
BALSAMIC VINEGAR DRESSING		
¼ cup	Balsamic vinegar	50 mL
½ tsp	salt (or more to taste)	2 mL
¼ tsp	freshly ground pepper	1 mL
1	clove garlic, minced	1
1 tsp	Dijon mustard	5 mL
4	anchovy fillets, mashed	4
¾ cup	extra-virgin olive oil	175 mL

1 Separate the cauliflower and broccoli into florets. Trim the tough bases off the asparagus and peel 1 in/2.5 cm up the stems. (If you are using beans, simply trim them.) Peel the carrots if necessary and cut into 2-in/5-cm sticks.

2 Cook each vegetable separately, until tender-crisp. Chill in ice water and pat dry with paper towels.

3 Arrange the vegetables in sections in a large dish. Slice the tomatoes into wedges and arrange beside the other vegetables with the fennel. Sprinkle with the olives and chopped basil.

4 Prepare the dressing by whisking the vinegar with the salt, pepper, garlic, mustard and anchovies. Whisk in the oil. Drizzle the dressing evenly over the vegetables and allow to marinate until ready to serve. (The salad can be eaten immediately, but will have a stronger taste if it is allowed to marinate for 1 to 2 hours.)

Tomatoes with Basil Parmesan Dressing

Serves 6

The most delicious Parmesan cheese is Parmigiano Reggiano. The cheese is sweet and not at all like some Parmesan cheese that is hard, bitter, salty and soapy.

Ripe tomatoes and fresh basil are the perfect way to welcome summer. If you cannot find fresh basil, use fresh parsley; do not substitute dry.

8	large ripe tomatoes	8
¼ cup	grated Parmesan cheese (preferably Parmigiano Reggiano)	50 mL
¼ cup	chopped fresh basil	50 mL
	Salt and freshly ground pepper to taste	
¼ cup	red wine vinegar or Balsamic vinegar	50 mL
¼ cup	extra-virgin olive oil	50 mL

1. Slice the tomatoes into slices ½ in/1 cm thick. Sprinkle with the cheese and basil.
2. Combine the salt, pepper, vinegar and oil and pour over the tomatoes.
3. Refrigerate for 1 hour or until serving time. Toss.

Potato Salad with Olives and Chopped Chives

Serves 6 to 8

Good potato salad is always a favourite. If you are making this salad a day ahead, by all means refrigerate it overnight. However, a warm potato salad, or one served at room temperature (that has never been refrigerated) has a special texture. Once potatoes are refrigerated, they tend to become slightly waxy. It's not that it matters—it's just different.

DRESSING	¼ cup	white wine winegar	50 mL
	1	clove garlic, minced	1
	2 tbsp	Dijon mustard	25 mL
	½ tsp	salt (or to taste)	2 mL
	¼ tsp	freshly ground pepper (or to taste)	1 mL
	½ cup	extra-virgin olive oil	125 mL
SALAD	3 lb	red-skinned potatoes or new potatoes	1.5 kg
	¼ cup	white wine vinegar	50 mL
	½ tsp	salt	2 mL
	½ cup	black olives	125 mL
	¼ cup	chopped fresh chives or green onions	50 mL
	3	hard-cooked eggs, cut into chunks	3

1. To prepare the dressing, combine ¼ cup/50 mL vinegar, garlic, mustard, salt and pepper in a bowl and whisk together. Whisk in the oil and taste the dressing. Adjust the seasonings if necessary.
2. Clean the potatoes and peel them. Cut them in half if they are large.
3. Place the potatoes in cold water with ¼ cup/50 mL vinegar and salt and bring to a boil. Simmer until tender, about 20 to 30 minutes.
4. As soon as the potatoes are cooked, drain well and toss with the dressing.
5. Add the olives, chives and eggs and allow to marinate until ready to serve, tossing occasionally. Serve warm or at room temperature.

SALADS AND SALAD DRESSINGS

New Wave Salad

Serves 6 to 8

"Designer" lettuces are very in vogue now. If they are hard to find, use this delicious dressing on Romaine or your favourite salad greens.

Boston lettuce is a tender green lettuce. Radicchio is approximately the same shape as Boston, but is much more compact and resembles a red cabbage. (Some people feel it's over-rated, but it can be delicious. At any rate, it's always pretty and always expensive). Ruby lettuce looks like leaf lettuce tinged with red. Belgian endive is becoming very popular (see pages 21 and 29) and is now widely available. And arugula, with its rocket-shaped leaves, is tangy and spicy-tasting.

	1	**small head Boston lettuce**	1
	1	**small head radicchio or ruby lettuce**	1
	2	**heads Belgian endive**	2
	1	**bunch arugula (sometimes called Rocket)**	1
DRESSING	3 tbsp	**red or white wine vinegar or raspberry vinegar**	50 mL
	3 tbsp	**whipping cream**	50 mL
	½ tsp	**salt**	2 mL
	¼ tsp	**freshly ground pepper**	1 mL
	⅓ cup	**extra-virgin olive oil (or more to taste)**	75 mL

1. Wash the lettuces well and break into bite-sized pieces. Dry them thoroughly and place in a salad bowl.
2. To make the dressing, place the vinegar in a bowl and whisk in the cream, salt and pepper. Whisk until frothy. Slowly beat in the oil. Taste and adjust the seasonings (the dressing should be creamy).
3. Just before serving, toss the lettuce with the dressing until well coated.

Salad Niçoise

Serves 6 to 8

This is a slightly off-beat version of Salad Niçoise. Instead of being in the salad, the tuna is pureed into a creamy dressing that is also delicious on cold chicken, veal or turkey.

DRESSING	1	50-g tin anchovies	1
	1	6½-oz/184-g tin tuna	1
	½ cup	mayonnaise, homemade (see page 111) or commercial	125 mL
	½ cup	sour cream (preferably Astro)	125 mL
SALAD	1	head Romaine lettuce	1
	5	potatoes, cooked and sliced	5
	1 lb	green beans, cooked	500 g
	4	tomatoes, cut into wedges	4
	3	hard-cooked eggs, chopped	3
	½ cup	black olives (preferably Kalamata)	125 mL
	1 tbsp	capers	15 mL
	2 tbsp	chopped fresh parsley	25 mL
	1 tsp	tarragon	5 mL
	3	green onions, chopped	3

1. Combine all the dressing ingredients in a blender or food processor. Taste and adjust seasonings if necessary.
2. Line a large salad bowl with the nicest lettuce leaves. Break up the remaining leaves and place in the bottom of the bowl.
3. Place the potato slices in the bowl and surround with the beans. Arrange the tomatoes and hard-cooked eggs around the outside edge of the salad.
4. Pour the dressing over the salad and sprinkle with the black olives, capers and herbs.

Leftover Steak Salad with Mustard Dressing

Serves 6

Dave Agar says nobody ever has leftover steak. However, if you do, it never tastes like the real thing again, so the best thing to do is turn it into something very different and delicious in its own right. Like this.

1 lb	cooked steak or roast beef (preferably rare)	500 g
3	medium boiling potatoes, cooked	3
1	red pepper, peeled*	1
1	yellow pepper, peeled*	1
6	green onions	6
4 oz	snow peas (optional)	125 g
	Any leftover cooked vegetables, such as asparagus, broccoli, beans, etc.	

MUSTARD DRESSING

¼ cup	red wine vinegar	50 mL
1 tbsp	Dijon mustard	15 mL
¾ cup	extra-virgin olive oil	175 mL
1 tsp	tarragon	5 mL
	Salt and freshly ground pepper to taste	

1. Slice the steak or roast beef thinly.
2. Slice the potatoes and add to the steak. Cut the red and yellow peppers into julienne pieces and add to the steak.
3. Chop the green onions. Toss gently with the steak and potato mixture.
4. If you are using snow peas, blanch them for 1 minute, chill in cold water and pat dry. Reserve for a garnish or combine with the salad. Add any cooked vegetables.
5. Combine the ingredients for the dressing. Season to taste. Mix gently into the salad and eat immediately or allow to marinate in the refrigerator for a few hours. This salad tastes best served almost at room temperature, so remove it from the refrigerator about 30 minutes before serving.

* *To peel peppers, simply use a potato peeler. Or char them under a broiler or on a barbecue, cool and remove the skins (see page 91).*

Smoked Chicken Salad

Serves 4 to 6

Smoked chicken is very popular now and easier to find. But smoked turkey or ham could be used instead in this recipe. My very favourite smoked chicken, turkey or ducks are made by Jack Kwinter in Toronto. This recipe could also be made with smoked salmon—use Honeycup or a Russian-style mustard instead of Dijon, and dill instead of basil.

	1 lb	potatoes (approximately 3 medium)	500 g
	1 lb	green beans or asparagus, cleaned and trimmed	500 g
	1 tsp	salt	5 mL
	3	eggs	3
	3	tomatoes	3
	1	head Romaine lettuce	1
	½	smoked chicken (approx. 1½ lb/750 g)	½
DRESSING	1 tbsp	Dijon mustard	15 mL
	3 tbsp	red wine vinegar	50 mL
	1 tsp	salt	5 mL
	¼ tsp	freshly ground pepper	1 mL
	½ cup	extra-virgin olive oil or corn oil	125 mL
	2 tbsp	chopped fresh basil or fresh parsley	25 mL

1. Bring a pot of water to the boil. Add the potatoes and cook for 30 to 35 minutes or until tender. Cool and slice.

2. Meanwhile, bring a deep skillet of water to the boil and add the asparagus or beans. Cook for 5 minutes. Drain and cool under cold water. Pat dry.

3. Bring a pot of water to the boil and add 1 tsp/5 mL salt. Add the eggs, reduce the heat and cook for 12 minutes. Cool under cold water and peel. Slice into quarters.

4. Slice the tomatoes and wash and dry the lettuce.

5. Remove the skin from the smoked chicken and separate the meat from the bones. Cut the meat into 1-in/2.5-cm pieces.

6. To assemble the salad, arrange the lettuce leaves over the bottom and up the sides of a large flat salad bowl. Arrange the potatoes in centre, the beans or asparagus around the potatoes, and the tomatoes around the outside edge. Place the chicken over the potatoes. Arrange the eggs around the chicken.

7. Prepare the dressing by whisking the mustard and vinegar together. Beat in 1 tsp/5 mL salt, pepper and then add the oil bit by bit. Add the basil. The dressing should be quite thick. Whisk again just before serving. Pour over the salad. Toss just before serving.

Cold Spaghetti Salad

Serves 8

Pasta salads have become very popular lately. This is one of my favourites. It is a terrific treat in summer for a light meal. (For more information on charring peppers, see page 91.)

4	**red peppers**	4
4	**yellow peppers**	4
4	**tomatoes, chopped**	4
2	**cloves garlic, minced**	2
¼ tsp	**hot red chili flakes**	1 mL
½ cup	**black olives (preferably Kalamata)**	125 mL
2 tbsp	**red wine vinegar**	25 mL
2 tbsp	**capers**	25 mL
4	**anchovies, minced**	4
½ cup	**extra-virgin olive oil**	125 mL
	Salt and freshly ground pepper to taste	
¼ cup	**chopped fresh basil or Italian parsley**	50 mL
1 lb	**spaghetti**	500 mL

1. Roast or broil the peppers until charred and blackened. Cool and peel off the skins. Seed and cut the peppers into julienned strips.

2. Place the peppers and tomatoes in a large bowl. Stir in the garlic, chili flakes, olives, vinegar, capers and anchovies. Mix well. Stir in the oil and season with salt and pepper. Add the basil.

3. Cook the spaghetti al dente. Drain and rinse with cold water. Combine well with the dressing. Taste and adjust seasonings. Serve cold or at room temperature.

Fennel and Black Olive Salad

Serves 6 to 8

Fennel is a fabulous, slightly anise- or licorice-flavoured vegetable. I like to use it with dips, in soups and salads. When it is cooked it becomes milder in flavour.

DRESSING	½ cup	black olives (preferably Kalamata)	125 mL
	1	anchovy fillet, minced	1
	1	clove garlic, minced	1
	1 tsp	capers, drained and chopped	5 mL
	2 tbsp	lemon juice	25 mL
	½ tsp	freshly ground pepper	2 mL
	½ cup	extra-virgin olive oil	125 mL
		Salt to taste	
	2 tbsp	chopped fresh basil or parsley	25 mL
SALAD	2	bulbs fennel, trimmed	2
	1	red onion	1
	¼ cup	slivered sun-dried tomatoes (optional)	50 mL
	1	head radicchio	1

1 Pit and mince 3 olives for the dressing. Reserve the remaining olives.

2 To make the dressing, combine the minced olives with all the remaining dressing ingredients using a whisk, or in a blender or food processor.

3 Slice the fennel and break apart into pieces.

4 Sliver the red onion and combine with the fennel, reserved olives and tomatoes.

5 Toss the vegetables with the dressing. Taste and adjust seasonings if necessary. Serve the salad on a bed of radicchio.

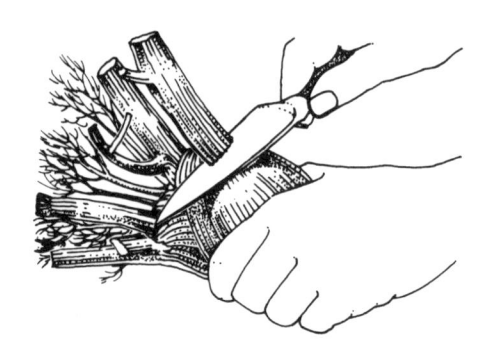

Vinaigrette

Makes ¾ cup/175 mL
(enough for salad for 8)

Although this is the most basic of all salad dressings, it probably is still the best. And there are many, many variations. Vinaigrette salad dressings are very easy to make, but it is important to use high-quality ingredients, because there are few ingredients and nothing to mask the flavours.

The best olive oil is extra virgin. It is made from the first pressing of the olives, which are usually cold pressed. For a sweet, smooth flavour, extra-virgin olive oil also contains less than one percent acidity. The best extra-virgin oils are made from olives that are naturally less than one percent acidity. Although extra-virgin oil is expensive, the cost is generally worth it. If you are not going to use the oil within a month, store it in the refrigerator. It will turn slightly cloudy and thicken, but don't worry. At room temperature it will be fine again. Make sure the salad greens are dried well before adding the dressing, and do not overdress. Toss very well until the dressing coats the greens.

The amount of oil you use in proportion to the vinegar is up to you. Most people love dressings they are served in restaurants (which have a high proportion of oil), but because of calorie fears are afraid to add a lot of oil when they are making salad dressings themselves.

Vinaigrette dressings are extremely popular right now and are even used warm over grilled foods or salads.

3 tbsp	vinegar (white or red wine, raspberry, Balsamic or herb, or lemon juice)	50 mL
1 tsp	dry mustard or Dijon mustard	5 mL
1 tsp	salt	5 mL
¼ tsp	freshly ground pepper	1 mL
8 to 12 tbsp	extra-virgin olive oil or vegetable oil of your choice	125 mL to 175 mL

1. Place the vinegar, mustard, salt and pepper in a bowl. Add the ingredients for any of the variations below if you wish.
2. Slowly whisk in the minimum amount of oil. Taste the dressing on a leaf of lettuce. Add more oil if necessary.
3. Toss well with salad greens just before serving.

VARIATIONS

Garlic Add a minced garlic clove.
Herb Add 2 tbsp/25 mL chopped fresh chives, basil, rosemary, chervil, parsley or tarragon (or a combination).
Mustard Add 1 tbsp/15 mL Dijon mustard instead of 1 tsp/5 mL.
Creamy Substitute 3 tbsp/50 mL whipping cream for 3 tbsp/50 mL oil.

Tarragon Salad Dressing

Makes ¾ cup/175 mL

This is a creamy-style, well-seasoned dressing. It is wonderful on lettuce, spinach or tomatoes. It also makes a great sauce for cold chicken breasts or cold sliced roast veal.

The oil you use is very important, as it is the largest ingredient. Taste the oil before using to make sure you like it on its own. If you add too much oil to the dressing, you can always adjust it with a little more vinegar. Toss the dressing with the greens just before serving. Use only enough dressing to coat leaves lightly. Don't drown them. (Extra dressing will keep in the refrigerator for a few days.)

1	egg yolk	1
3 tbsp	red wine vinegar	50 mL
1 tsp	dry mustard	5 mL
1 tsp	salt	5 mL
¼ tsp	freshly ground pepper	1 mL
1	small clove garlic, minced (optional)	1
1 tsp	dried tarragon (or 1 tbsp/15 mL fresh)	5 mL
1 tbsp	chopped fresh parsley	15 mL
¾ cup	extra-virgin olive oil or favourite vegetable oil	175 mL

1. By hand with a whisk, or in a blender or food processor, combine the egg yolk with the vinegar, mustard, salt, pepper, garlic, tarragon and parsley.

2. Very slowly, whisking constantly, drip in the oil. After adding ⅔ cup/150 mL oil, taste the dressing on a leaf of lettuce and, if it is too tart, add more oil.

Homemade Mayonnaise

Makes 1½ cups/375 mL

This is so much better than store-bought, and it is easy to prepare. All the ingredients should be at room temperature.

If the mayonnaise curdles or does not thicken, simply pour the mixture into a measuring cup, add a fresh egg to the machine and drip the curdled sauce into the egg while the machine is running.

2	**egg yolks or 1 whole egg (room temperature)**	2
1 tsp	**dry mustard**	5 mL
	Salt and freshly ground pepper to taste	
pinch	**cayenne pepper**	pinch
3 tbsp	**lemon juice or red wine vinegar**	50 mL
1¼ cups	**oil (a combination of extra-virgin olive oil and vegetable oil)**	300 mL

1. Place the egg yolks, mustard, salt, pepper, cayenne, lemon juice and ¼ cup/50 mL oil in a blender or food processor. Combine well.

2. While the machine is running, slowly drip the remaining oil into the egg mixture. The more oil you add, the thicker the mayonnaise will become.

VARIATIONS

Curry Mayonnaise   Add 1 to 2 tsp/5 to 10 mL curry powder to the finished mayonnaise. Use it over cold poached chicken.

Dill Mayonnaise   Add ⅓ cup/75 mL chopped fresh dill to the finished mayonnaise. It is great with shrimp or crab.

Sweet Mustard Mayonnaise   Add 2 tbsp/25 mL Russian-style mustard (my favourite is Honeycup). This is delicious with any smoked salmon, chicken or ham salad or sandwiches.

Breads and Muffins

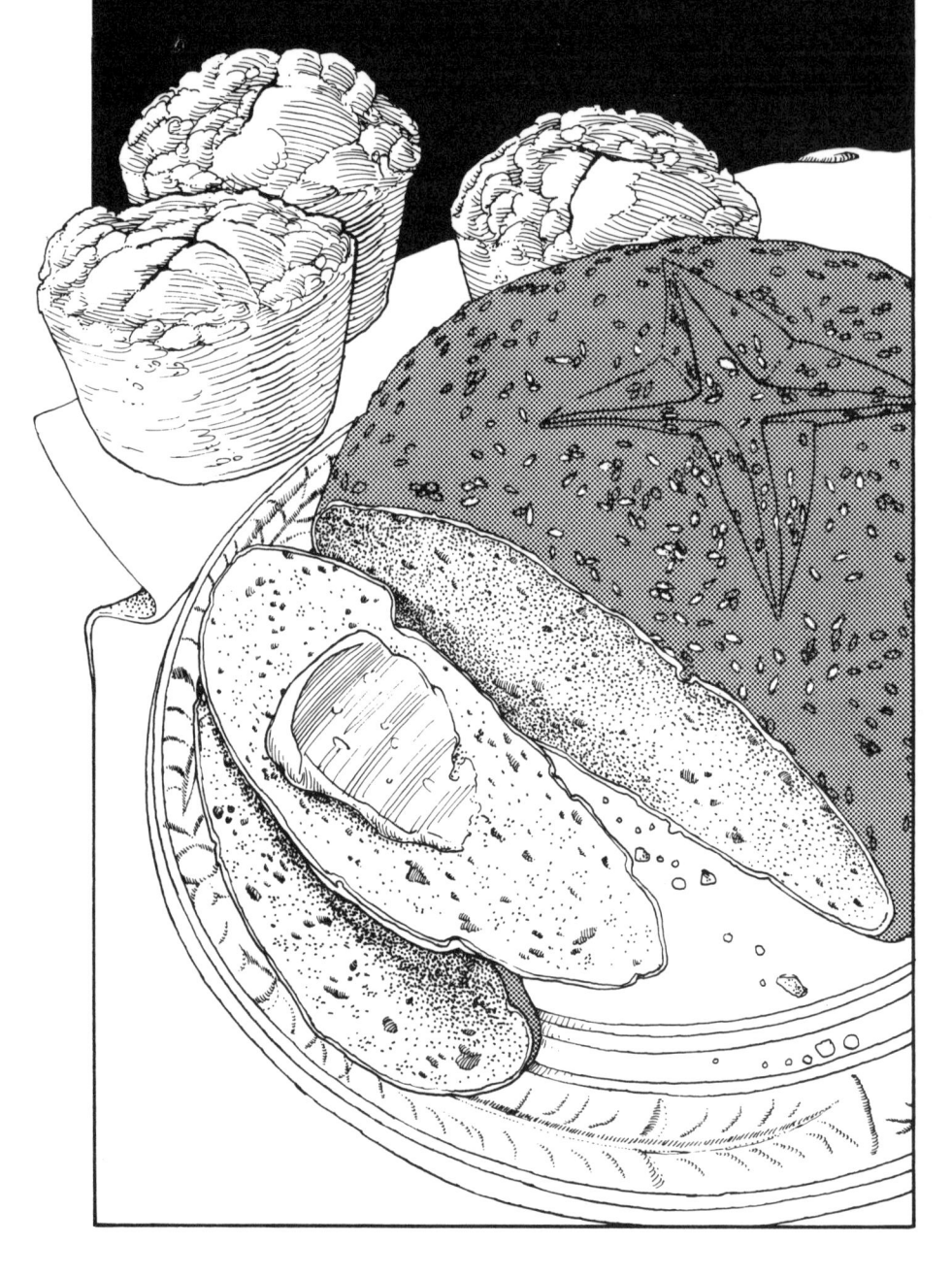

Cornbread with Cheese Custard Filling

Serves 4 to 6

With North American cooking becoming so popular, recipes for cornbread abound. There are many different styles of cornbread, as well as different ingredient variations and cooking methods. This one is moist and cheesy and slightly spicy because of the green chilies.

Lynn Pickering, associate producer of "Hour Toronto Magazine", loves this recipe so much that she says she makes it about once a week. Should we believe her? Try it and see!

¾ cup	grated old Cheddar cheese	175 mL
1	4-oz/110-g tin chopped green chilies	1
2 tbsp	chopped pitted black olives	25 mL
⅔ cup	unflavoured yogurt (preferably Astro)	150 mL
1 cup	all-purpose flour	250 mL
2 tbsp	sugar	25 mL
4 tsp	baking powder	20 mL
1 cup	yellow cornmeal	250 mL
½ tsp	salt	2 mL
2	eggs	2
1 cup	milk	250 mL
¼ cup	unsalted butter, melted	50 mL

1. Preheat the oven to 400°F/200°C. Butter an 8-in/1.5-L baking dish.
2. Combine the cheese with the chilies, olives and yogurt and reserve.
3. Combine the flour, sugar, baking powder, cornmeal and salt.
4. Combine the eggs, milk and melted butter.
5. Stir the egg mixture into the flour mixture just until combined. Pour into the prepared pan. Pour the cheese mixture on top and swirl it into the batter.
6. Bake for 25 to 30 minutes until the top is golden brown and puffed. Serve warm.

Mostly Whole Wheat Bread

Makes 2 loaves

If you use only whole wheat flour in bread, your bread will have a wonderful nutty flavour but may be quite dense. Therefore I prefer to combine whole wheat and all-purpose flour. I like the whole wheat flour for its flavour and healthful qualities and the all-purpose for its texture.

Most cooks agree that bread is the most rewarding food they can make. It's warm, homey and delicious, and makes you feel like Mother Earth.

1 tbsp	sugar		15 mL
½ cup	warm water		125 mL
2	packages dry yeast		2
2 cups	milk		500 mL
1 tbsp	salt		15 mL
⅓ cup	honey		75 mL
¼ cup	vegetable oil		50 mL
3 cups	all-purpose or hard unbleached flour (more if necessary)		750 mL
3 cups	hard whole wheat flour		750 mL
½ cup	wheat germ		125 mL
¼ cup	bran or cracked wheat (optional)		50 mL
GLAZE			
1	egg		1
1 tbsp	water		15 mL

1. Dissolve the sugar in the warm water and sprinkle with the yeast. Allow to rest for 10 minutes. The yeast should bubble up and double in volume. If this does not happen, the water was too hot or the yeast was too old. Start again with cooler water or buy fresh yeast.

2. Heat the milk, salt, honey and oil until the salt has dissolved. Cool to lukewarm.

3. Combine the dry ingredients in a large bowl. When the yeast has doubled, stir it down and add it to the flour.

4. Add the milk mixture and combine the ingredients well. (The dough may need a bit more flour if it is too sticky.)

5. Sprinkle the work surface with flour and knead the dough until it is satiny, about 10 minutes. If you have a mixmaster that is strong enough for bread dough, knead for about 7 minutes.

6. Butter a large bowl and turn the dough around in it so that all sides are greasy. Cover the bowl with plastic wrap and then a tea towel. Set it in a warm place to rise until doubled in bulk, about 1½ hours.

7. Punch the dough down and divide it in half. Roll each half into a rectangle and roll up tightly to fit 2 8-in x 4-in/1.5-L bread pans. Butter the pans and place the dough in them to rise a final time, about 1 hour. (The loaves should be loosely covered and in a warm place.)

8. Preheat the oven to 400°F/200°C. Combine the egg and water to make the glaze. Brush the loaves with the glaze and bake for 30 to 40 minutes. Remove the bread from the pans and cool on racks. Don't eat it all at once!

Apricot Almond Quickbread

Makes one 9-in x 5-in/2 L loaf

This recipe is so easy and fast that it's hard to believe it can be so delicious.
To toast the almonds, spread them on a cookie sheet and bake at 350° F/180° C for 5 to 10 minutes or until light brown.
The easiest way to chop dried apricots is to cut them with scissors.

¾ cup	dried apricots	175 mL
1 cup	boiling water	250 mL
2 cups	all-purpose flour	500 mL
1 tbsp	baking powder	15 mL
¾ cup	granulated sugar	175 mL
½ cup	sliced toasted almonds	125 mL
2	eggs	2
1 cup	milk	250 mL
⅓ cup	unsalted butter, melted	75 mL
¼ tsp	pure almond extract	1 mL
½ tsp	pure vanilla extract	2 mL

1 Preheat oven to 350°F/180°C.

2 Chop dried apricots. Place them in a bowl and cover with the boiling water. Allow them to rest for 10 minutes while preparing the batter.

3 Combine the flour, baking powder and sugar. Stir together well. Stir in the almonds.

4 Combine the eggs, milk, melted butter and extracts. Pour the wet ingredients over the dry ingredients and stir only until blended.

5 Drain the apricots and pat dry with paper towels. Stir them into the batter. Spoon the mixture into a buttered 8-inch x 4-inch/1.5-L loaf pan and bake for 1 hour. Allow the loaf to rest in the pan for 10 minutes before inverting onto a wire rack to cool.

Apple Oatmeal Bread

Makes 2 loaves

One of my students, Dick Dewhurst, taught me the delicious trick of cooking oats in apple juice. It's delicious as oatmeal and also wonderful when the leftovers are made into bread.

1 tsp	granulated sugar	5 mL
½ cup	warm water	125 mL
1	package dry yeast	1
2 cups	oatmeal cooked in apple juice (or any cooked cereal), warm*	500 mL
¼ cup	unsalted butter, melted, or vegetable oil	50 mL
1½ tsp	salt	7 mL
¼ cup	brown sugar	50 mL
½ cup	bran	125 mL
1 cup	hard whole wheat flour	250 mL
4 cups	all-purpose flour (approximately)	1 L
GLAZE		
1	egg	1
¼ tsp	salt	1 mL

1. Dissolve the granulated sugar in the warm water and sprinkle with yeast. Allow to rest for 10 minutes, or until doubled in volume and bubbly.

2. Combine the oatmeal with the butter, salt and brown sugar. Stir to dissolve and combine the ingredients well. Stir in the dissolved yeast.

3. Combine the bran with the whole wheat flour and 2 cups/500 mL all-purpose flour. Stir in the oatmeal-yeast mixture. Add additional flour (do this by hand, in a heavy-duty mixer or a large food processor) until the dough is soft and manageable, but not too sticky. (Knead for 10 minutes by hand, 5 minutes in a mixer and 1 minute in the food processor.)

4. Place the dough in a well-buttered bowl, cover and allow to rise in a warm place for 1½ to 2 hours or until doubled in bulk.

5. Punch the dough down and divide in two. Roll each piece into a rectangle and roll up to fit the loaf pans. Place the loaves in 2 8-in x 4-in/1.5-L loaf pans that have been buttered and lined with parchment paper. Cover with buttered plastic wrap and allow to rise in a warm place for 1 to 1½ hours until doubled.

6. Preheat the oven to 400°F/200°C.

7. Combine the egg with the salt and brush the loaves with this glaze. Bake for 35 to 45 minutes. Remove from the pans and cool on wire racks.

* *If you don't have quite enough oatmeal, make up the difference with apple juice or milk. To make the cereal cook 1 cup/250 mL oats and 2 cups/500 mL apple juice for 5 minutes.*

Banana Blueberry Muffins *Makes 12 large muffins*

Oat bran has recently been touted as the new healthful ingredient of our times. It can be added to breads, muffins, hamburgers or toppings for crisps. It has a wonderful oat flavour.

2 cups	all-purpose flour	500 mL
¼ cup	oat bran	50 mL
¼ tsp	salt	1 mL
2 tsp	baking powder	10 mL
¼ tsp	baking soda	1 mL
	Grated peel of 1 orange	
½ cup	brown sugar	125 mL
⅓ cup	unsalted butter, melted	75 mL
1	small ripe banana, mashed	1
½ tsp	pure vanilla extract	2 mL
2	eggs	2
1 cup	buttermilk	250 mL
1 cup	blueberries, fresh or frozen	250 mL

1. Preheat the oven to 400°F/200°C. Butter 12 large muffin pans.
2. Combine the dry ingredients together in a bowl.
3. Combine the melted butter with the mashed banana, vanilla, eggs and buttermilk.
4. Pour the wet ingredients on top of the dry ingredients and combine just until mixed. Stir in the blueberries (if you are using frozen blueberries, make sure they have been patted dry).
5. Spoon the batter into the buttered pans and bake for 25 to 30 minutes.

Brioche

Makes 12 small loaves

Brioche is a luxurious, rich French breakfast bread. It is not at all hard to prepare (but tastes as if it is!). It makes a great snack and is also perfect to serve for brunch. Leftovers can be used to make wonderfully rich bread puddings, fabulous French toast and exquisite "melba"-type toast to use for hors d'oeuvre.

Classic brioche pans are the fluted ones shown below, but you can also bake the dough in loaves for use as toast or in sandwiches and canapés.

2 tsp	sugar	10 mL
½ cup	warm milk	125 mL
1	package dry yeast	1
4 cups	all-purpose flour	1 L
1½ tsp	salt	7 mL
2 tbsp	sugar	25 mL
3	eggs	3
2	egg yolks	2
¾ cup	unsalted butter, at room temperature	175 mL
GLAZE 1	egg	1
½ tsp	salt	2 mL

1. Dissolve 2 tsp/10 mL sugar in the warm milk and sprinkle the yeast on top. Allow to rest for 10 minutes or until the yeast bubbles up.

2. In a large bowl (or bowl of a mixer with a dough hook), combine 2½ cups/625 mL flour with the salt and 2 tbsp/25 mL sugar. Mix well.

3. Beat the eggs and egg yolks together. Stir down the yeast and add to the eggs. Stir the egg mixture into the flour mixture by hand or with the mixer. (The dough should be sticky.)

4. Beat in the butter and add extra flour until the dough can just be handled without sticking too much. The trick is not to add too much flour, but you must be able to knead the dough a little. If mixing by hand, knead for about 5 minutes with floured hands. In a mixer, beat for 3 to 4 minutes.

5. Place the dough in a buttered bowl (turn the dough over to coat completely with the butter), cover with plastic wrap and allow to rise for 1 hour at room temperature or until the dough has doubled in bulk.

6. Punch the dough down, knead slightly and place in the bowl again. Cover and allow to rise in the refrigerator overnight or even for a few days, if you do not plan to use dough right away.

7 To shape brioche for small buns, divide the dough into 12 pieces. Break off about one-eighth of each piece for the topknot. Shape the large piece into a nice ball and place in a buttered brioche pan. Shape each small piece into a pear shape. With scissors, cut a cross into the top of each bun, as shown. Insert the pointed end of the pear piece in the slit. Push together gently. Cover loosely with buttered plastic wrap and allow to rise in a warm place for about 1½ hours or until doubled in bulk.
8 Preheat the oven to 400°F/200°C.
9 Beat the egg and salt together and brush on top of the brioches. Bake for 15 to 20 minutes. Remove from the pans and cool on racks.

Food Processor Method: If you are making these in the food processor, have the butter cold. Add the dry ingredients to the work bowl as in Step 2, using only 2½ cups/625 mL flour. Add the cold butter in bits to the flour and process until the butter is in tiny pieces. Beat the eggs with the yolks and yeast mixture. With the machine running, slowly drizzle the liquid ingredients into the dry ingredients. (The mixture should be quite sticky!) Add enough flour for the dough to clean the sides of the work bowl (the dough should still be moist). Knead for 1 minute. Continue as in Step 5.

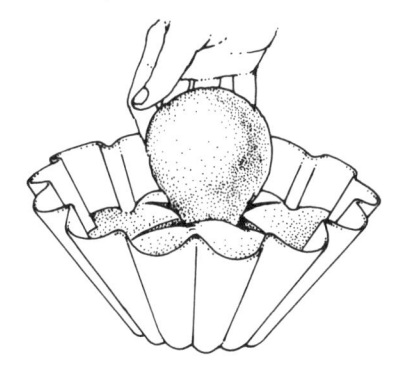

Labour of Love Sticky Buns

Makes 15 to 18 buns

This recipe is dedicated to Dr. Shime at Toronto General Hospital. When I was in labour with my son, Mark, the doctor told me to keep busy, so I made these buns. When they were ready, I went to the hospital. My husband and Dr. Shime ate the buns for breakfast!

(Note: When I was preparing this recipe, I lay down on the floor every ten minutes and had a contraction, but if you are not in labour, this is not necessary!)

DOUGH

1 tbsp	sugar	15 mL
¼ cup	warm water	50 mL
1	package dry yeast	1
2 cups	milk	500 mL
¼ cup	sugar	50 mL
2 tsp	salt	10 mL
¼ cup	unsalted butter	50 mL
6 cups	all-purpose flour (approximately)	1.5 L

FILLING

1 cup	unsalted butter, at room temperature (or more)	250 mL
2 cups	light brown sugar (or more)	500 mL
2 tbsp	cinnamon	25 mL
½ cup	chopped toasted walnuts	125 mL
½ cup	raisins	125 mL

1. Dissolve 1 tbsp/15 mL sugar in the warm water and sprinkle dry yeast over it. Allow to rest for 10 minutes or until the mixture bubbles up and doubles in volume.

2. Meanwhile, combine the milk, ¼ cup/50 mL sugar, salt and butter and heat until the butter melts. Stir until the salt and sugar have dissolved. Cool to lukewarm.

3. Place 4 cups/1 L flour in a large bowl. Stir the yeast and combine it with the lukewarm milk mixture. Stir into the flour and combine well. (The mixture will probably be very sticky.) Keep adding more flour until the dough can be handled. (Do not worry if you need less or more than 6 cups/1.5 L flour. The dough should be nice and soft but not so sticky that it sticks to your fingers.) Knead the dough for about 5 minutes. (This can be made in a heavy-duty mixmaster with the dough hook, or in a large food processor with the plastic blade. Knead for 3 minutes in a mixmaster or 30 seconds in a food processor.)

4. Place the dough in a well-buttered bowl and turn so that the dough is well greased all over. Cover with plastic wrap and allow to rise in a warm, cosy spot for 1 to 1½ hours, or until doubled in bulk.

5 Punch the dough down and divide in half. Roll each half out into a large rectangle, about ¼ inch/5 mm thick. Spread each rectangle generously with butter. Then sprinkle generously with brown sugar and cinnamon.
6 Sprinkle the nuts and raisins over both halves. Roll up each rectangle lengthwise. Cut into 1½-in/4-cm pieces.
7 Generously butter a 9-in x 13-in/3-L baking dish. Sprinkle generously with brown sugar. Arrange the rolls side by side in the dish with the spiral side facing up. Cover with buttered plastic wrap and allow to rise in a warm, cosy place for about 1 hour or until the dough has doubled in size.
8 Preheat the oven to 400°F/200°C. Bake the buns for 30 to 40 minutes. Turn out of the pan as soon as you remove them from the oven and allow the syrup to run all over them.

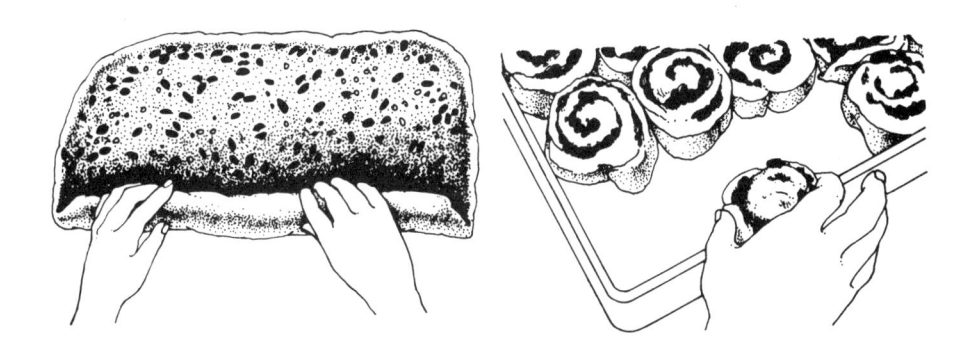

Fresh Date and Yogurt Muffins

Makes 12 extra-large muffins

I have been delighted to see fresh dates available in some Toronto food stores. They're delicious to eat on their own. If you can't find fresh ones, just substitute dried. Try using an ice-cream scoop to scoop muffin batter into the pans. It gives the muffins nicely rounded tops.

1½ cups	fresh dates, pitted and diced (or 1 cup/250 mL dried)	375 mL
½ cup	chopped toasted walnuts	125 mL
2 cups	bran	500 mL
1½ cups	all-purpose flour	375 mL
1½ tsp	baking powder	7 mL
1½ tsp	baking soda	7 mL
pinch	salt	pinch
½ cup	vegetable oil	125 mL
1 cup	brown sugar	250 mL
2	eggs	2
1½ cups	unflavoured yogurt (preferably Astro)	375 mL

1. Preheat the oven to 400°F/200°C. Butter 12 extra-large muffin pans.
2. Mix the dates and nuts with the bran, flour, baking powder, baking soda and salt.
3. Combine the oil with the sugar, eggs and yogurt.
4. Stir the wet ingredients into the dry ingredients, just until blended. Scoop into muffin pans and bake for 20 to 30 minutes.

Cornbread Muffins

Makes 12 medium or 8 large muffins

The last time I was in California, every restaurant I visited served some form of cornbread. And why not? It only takes a minute to make, and you get to serve homemade bread. It's a great idea—try it at home.

¾ cup	yellow cornmeal	175 mL
1 cup	all-purpose flour	250 mL
¼ cup	sugar	50 mL
1 tbsp	baking powder	15 mL
¼ tsp	salt	1 mL
1	egg, lightly beaten	1
1 cup	milk	250 mL
¼ cup	unsalted butter, melted	50 mL

1. Preheat the oven to 425°F/210°C. Butter the muffin pans or line with paper muffin cups.
2. Combine the cornmeal, flour, sugar, baking powder and salt. Stir well.
3. Combine the egg, milk and melted butter. Stir into the dry mixture and combine just until blended.
4. Scoop the filling into the prepared muffin pans. Bake for 20 to 25 minutes.

Orange Pecan Muffins

Makes 18 medium muffins

The orange flavour is terrific in these delicious, healthful muffins. They are quite dense, but full of good things.

2 cups	all-purpose flour	500 mL
1 cup	wheat bran	250 mL
½ cup	oat bran	125 mL
1½ tsp	baking soda	7 mL
1½ tsp	baking powder	7 mL
½ tsp	salt	2 mL
1 tsp	cinnamon	5 mL
1 cup	brown sugar	250 mL
½ cup	unsalted butter, melted, or vegetable oil	125 mL
2	eggs	2
1¼ cups	unflavoured yogurt (preferably Astro)	300 mL
¼ cup	frozen orange juice concentrate	50 mL
2 tbsp	grated orange peel	25 mL
¾ cup	coarsely chopped toasted pecans	175 mL

1. Preheat the oven to 400°F/200°C. Butter the muffin pans well.
2. Combine the dry ingredients together in a bowl. Combine the butter, eggs, yogurt and orange juice.
3. Stir the yogurt mixture into the dry ingredients until barely blended. Quickly stir in the orange peel and nuts.
4. Spoon the batter into the prepared pans and bake for 20 to 25 minutes.

Cakes

Mocha Trifle Cake

Serves 12

Most of the time, an Italian meal is completed with fruit and cheese. But there are some spectacular Italian desserts served on special occasions. This is one of them. This cake freezes well, but I like to decorate it with the cream just before serving. If you don't care about the "bomba" shape, simply assemble the layers in a regular round or square cake shape.

	1	All-purpose Sponge Cake (see page 128), baked in three 9-in/24-cm layer pans or one 9-in/24-cm springform pan and cut horizontally into three layers	1
	½ cup	rum	125 mL
FILLING	1 cup	unsalted butter	250 mL
	2 cups	sifted icing sugar	500 mL
	3	egg yolks	3
	⅓ cup	extra-strong coffee	75 mL
	1 tbsp	Amaretto	15 mL
	¾ cup	chopped bittersweet or semisweet chocolate	175 mL
	1 cup	chopped toasted almonds	250 mL
ICING	1½ cups	whipping cream	375 mL
	2 tbsp	sugar	25 mL
	1 tbsp	rum	15 mL
	1 tbsp	Amaretto	15 mL
	1 tbsp	cocoa	15 mL

1. Cut one layer of sponge cake into eight wedges. Line a bomba-shaped 4-qt/4-L mixing bowl (about 9 in/24 cm in diameter) with plastic wrap, as shown. Cut one of the remaining cake layers to fit into the bottom of the bowl. Reserve the scraps. Wedge the eight wedges up the sides. (Do not worry if it is not perfect because the whole thing will eventually be iced.) Sprinkle the cake with rum.

2. For the filling, beat the butter until it is light and fluffy. Gradually beat in the sugar and continue beating until very light. Add the egg yolks one at a time and keep beating. Add the coffee and Amaretto, and then fold in the chocolate and nuts.

3. Spoon half the filling into the cake-lined bowl. Arrange the extra scraps of cake (from the second layer) on top. Sprinkle with rum. Cover with the remaining filling and then top with the third cake layer, which should just cover everything nicely. Sprinkle with the remaining rum. Cover with plastic wrap and refrigerate overnight.

4. To make the icing, whip the cream until light. Beat in the liqueurs.

CAKES

5 Line a serving plate with strips of waxed paper. Unwrap the bomba and unmould. Spread some cream over the bomba. Use the remaining cream to pipe over the cake. Dust with cocoa. Remove the waxed paper and refrigerate until ready to serve.

All-purpose Sponge Cake

Makes one round 9-in/24-cm springform cake

This is a delicious sponge cake that can be used for trifle (see page 148), cakes (see page 126) or whenever you want a plain, light, but really good cake. It can also be baked as a jelly roll, but reduce the baking time to 20 to 25 minutes.

1 cup	cake and pastry flour	250 mL
¼ tsp	baking powder	1 mL
pinch	salt	pinch
3	eggs, separated	3
⅓ cup	ice water	75 mL
1 cup	sugar	250 mL
¼ tsp	pure almond extract	1 mL
½ tsp	pure vanilla extract	2 mL
¼ tsp	cream of tartar	1 mL

1. Preheat the oven to 325°F/160°C. Line an ungreased 9-in/24-cm springform pan with a round of parchment paper or waxed paper.
2. Sift together the flour, baking powder and salt. Reserve.
3. Beat the egg yolks until thick and lemony. Beat in the ice water until pale and foamy.
4. Add the sugar and beat until the mixture is very light and the sugar is dissolved, about 10 minutes with an electric beater. Add the extracts.
5. Fold the flour into the yolk mixture in three additions.
6. Beat the egg whites and cream of tartar until light. Fold the egg whites into the batter.
7. Turn the batter gently into the pan and bake for 40 to 50 minutes. Cool on a rack before removing from the pan.

Peach Upside-Down Cake

Makes one 8-in/20-cm square cake

This is an old-fashioned, friendly dessert. And easy!
If the peaches are difficult to peel, cook them in boiling water for 1 minute. Rinse in cold water before peeling.

BASE	¼ cup	unsalted butter	50 mL
	1 cup	firmly packed brown sugar	250 mL
	4	medium peaches	4
CAKE	½ cup	unsalted butter, melted	125 mL
	½ cup	milk	125 mL
	1	egg	1
	1 tsp	pure vanilla extract	5 mL
	½ tsp	cinnamon	2 mL
	pinch	nutmeg	pinch
	1½ cups	all-purpose flour	375 mL
	½ cup	granulated sugar	125 mL
	2 tsp	baking powder	10 mL
	pinch	salt	pinch

1 Preheat the oven to 400°F/200°C.

2 To make the base, place ¼ cup/50 mL butter in 8-in/20-cm square baking pan and place in the oven for 5 minutes or until melted. Add the brown sugar, stir and return to the oven until the sugar melts, about another 5 minutes.

3 Meanwhile, peel and slice the peaches. Arrange on top of the brown-sugar mixture. Add any juices accumulated while handling the peaches.

4 To make the cake, combine the melted butter, milk and egg. Add the vanilla, cinnamon and nutmeg.

5 Sift the dry ingredients together. Add the milk mixture to the flour mixture and stir only until barely combined.

6 Spread the cake batter over the peaches. Bake for 35 minutes. Allow the cake to rest for 5 minutes. Invert onto a serving plate. Serve warm or cold.

Fruitcake with Amaretto

Makes 6 to 7 small loaf cakes
5½ in x 3 in x 1½ in/250 mL

Linda Stephen, who has taught many wonderful classes at my school, developed this recipe for our Gifts from the Kitchen course. This has become more or less "fruitcake update" for most of my students. Even people who don't normally like fruitcake will love this recipe.

⅓ cup	Amaretto	75 mL
¼ cup	golden raisins	50 mL
¼ cup	dark raisins	50 mL
1 lb	unsalted butter	500 g
2¼ cups	sugar	550 mL
7	eggs	7
½ tsp	pure almond extract	2 mL
3½ cups	all-purpose flour	875 mL
½ tsp	salt	2 mL
1 tbsp	grated lemon peel	15 mL
1 tbsp	grated orange peel	15 mL
¾ cup	diced dried apricots (approx. 4 oz/125 g)	175 mL
1¼ cups	candied mixed peel (approx. 8 oz/250 g)	300 mL
⅓ cup	candied citron (approx. 2 oz/60 g)	75 mL
¾ cup	grated bittersweet or semisweet chocolate (approx. 4 oz/125 g)	175 mL

1 Pour the Amaretto over both kinds of raisins and allow to rest for 1 hour. Butter the loaf pans, line with parchment paper and butter again.

2 Preheat the oven to 325°F/160°C.

3 Beat 1 lb/500 g butter until light. Gradually beat in the sugar. Add the eggs, two at a time, beating well after each addition. Add the almond extract with the last egg.

4 Combine the flour with the salt and stir into the batter. Do not overmix. Mix in the raisins and all the remaining ingredients.

5 Spoon the batter into the prepared pans. Bake for 50 minutes or until a cake tester inserted in the centre of a loaf comes out clean.

6 Allow the cakes to cool for 15 minutes in the pans before unmoulding. Cool completely on racks. Wrap in foil and store in the refrigerator.

Note: If you wish a more traditionally flavoured fruitcake, add to the flour 1 tsp/5 mL cinnamon, 1 tsp/5 mL allspice, ½ tsp/2 mL nutmeg and ½ tsp/2 mL cloves.

Ray's Square Apple Pie Cake

Serves 8 to 10

My husband loves apples and is always trying to get me to recreate his favourite childhood dessert. His clues are, "It's not really a pie, it's not really a cake, it's not really a crisp." I have not been successful yet, but he loves me more each time I try. "This version is getting close," he says.

CRUST	2 cups	all-purpose flour	500 mL
	2 tbsp	granulated sugar	25 mL
	pinch	salt	pinch
	¾ cup	unsalted butter, cold	175 mL
	1	egg, cold, lightly beaten	1
	2 tbsp	ice water	25 mL
FILLING	6	apples (Spy or Golden Delicious)	6
	⅓ cup	all-purpose flour	75 mL
	⅓ cup	brown sugar	75 mL
	½ tsp	cinnamon	2 mL
	2 tbsp	unsalted butter, cold, cut into bits	25 mL
GLAZE	1	egg	1
	1 tbsp	granulated sugar	15 mL

1 To make the crust, combine 2 cups/500 mL flour with 2 tbsp/25 mL granulated sugar and salt. Cut ¾ cup/175 mL butter into small pieces and cut into the flour until the mixture resembles fresh breadcrumbs.

2 Beat the egg with the water and add to the flour. Gather the dough together to form a ball. Wrap and refrigerate while preparing the filling.

3 To make the filling, peel the apples, cut them in half and remove the cores. Slice or dice and place in a large bowl. Combine ⅓ cup/75 mL flour, brown sugar, cinnamon and 3 tbsp/25 mL butter and combine well with the apples. Reserve.

4 Preheat the oven to 400°F/200°C. Divide the dough in two pieces. Roll out one piece to fit the bottom of a 9-in x 13-in/3-L baking pan. Press or roll the dough into the bottom. Spread the apples on top. Roll out the remaining dough and fit over the top. Pierce with a fork.

5 To make the glaze, beat the egg lightly and brush over the top crust. Sprinkle with 1 tbsp/15 mL granulated sugar. Bake for 1 hour. (Check after 30 minutes and if the top crust is browning too much, reduce the heat to 350°F/180°C.)

Anna Banana's Birthday Cake
(Banana Cake with Chocolate Fudge Icing)

Makes one 9-in/24-cm cake

Everyone calls my daughter Anna Banana, and she happens to adore bananas! Therefore it was only natural to have a banana theme party for her first birthday. Everyone dressed in yellow, we had a clown dressed as a banana as entertainment, the food and table settings were all banana related or yellow, and we gave yellow loot bags that all had bananas in them. I made this cake in the shape of a heart. I wrote Happy Birthday in bright yellow on the chocolate fudge icing and made little perfect marzipan bananas for decorations. It really was sweet.

Since this recipe was given on air, we have received lots of letters to say that many listeners have been having yellow and/or banana birthday parties, with great success!

CAKE	½ cup	unsalted butter	125 mL
	¾ cup	granulated sugar	175 mL
	2	eggs	2
	1 tsp	pure vanilla extract	5 mL
	3	ripe bananas, mashed	3
	2 cups	all-purpose flour	500 mL
	1 tsp	baking soda	5 mL
	¼ cup	sour cream (preferably Astro)	50 mL
CHOCOLATE FUDGE ICING			
	4 oz	bittersweet or semisweet chocolate	125 g
	2 tbsp	cocoa (preferably Dutch processed)	25 mL
	⅓ cup	milk	75 mL
	¼ cup	unsalted butter	50 mL
	1½ cups	sifted icing sugar (more if needed)	375 mL
	1 tsp	pure vanilla extract	5 mL

1 Preheat the oven to 350°F/180°C. Butter a 9-in/24-cm springform pan (or heart-shaped pan).

2 Cream ½ cup/125 mL butter until light. Gradually beat in the granulated sugar.

3 Add the eggs one at a time and beat after each addition. Beat in 1 tsp/5 mL vanilla and the mashed bananas.

4 Sift or mix together the dry ingredients and add to the batter alternately with the sour cream. Spoon the batter into the prepared pan evenly and bake for 30 to 40 minutes or until the cake springs back when gently pressed in the centre. Cool for 10 minutes and invert. Cool on a wire rack.

5 For the icing, melt the chocolate, cocoa, milk and ¼ cup/50 mL butter in the top of a double boiler. Cook until smooth and cool slightly.

6 Beat in the icing sugar and 1 tsp/5 mL vanilla. Place the bowl over a larger bowl of ice and water and stir until the icing is spreadable.

7 Ice the cake and decorate as you wish.

Mud Cake with Fudge Glaze

Makes 1 large tube cake

Everyone loves a good chocolate cake. This one is fudgy and rich and is baked in a tube pan for a slightly different look.

CAKE	1¼ cups	all-purpose flour	300 mL
	1 tsp	baking powder	5 mL
	½ tsp	baking soda	2 mL
	pinch	salt	pinch
	2 oz	unsweetened chocolate, chopped	60 g
	3 tbsp	cocoa	50 mL
	½ cup	boiling water	125 mL
	½ cup	unsalted butter, at room temperature	125 mL
	1 cup	granulated sugar	250 mL
	2	eggs	2
	½ tsp	pure vanilla extract	2 mL
	½ cup	sour cream (preferably Astro)	125 mL
FUDGE GLAZE			
	4 oz	bittersweet chocolate	125 g
	2 tbsp	cocoa	25 mL
	⅓ cup	whipping cream	150 mL
	¼ cup	unsalted butter, at room temperature	50 mL
	1¼ cups	icing sugar, sifted	300 mL

1 Preheat the oven to 350°F/180°C. Butter a large 10-cup/2.5-L tube pan.

2 To make the cake, sift together the flour, baking powder, baking soda and salt. Reserve.

3 Place the chopped chocolate and cocoa in a bowl. Pour the boiling water over and allow the chocolate to sit for about 2 minutes. Stir to complete the melting.

4 Cream the butter until light. Add the granulated sugar gradually and beat until light.

5 Add the eggs one at a time and beat after each addition. Blend in the chocolate, vanilla and sour cream.

6 Add the dry ingredients and blend together briefly just until combined.

7 Transfer the batter to the prepared pan and bake for 35 to 40 minutes. Do not overbake. Cool for 10 minutes in the pan and then invert onto a rack. Cool.

8 To prepare the glaze, place the chocolate, cocoa and cream in the top of a double boiler over simmering water and cook until melted and smooth. Remove from heat.

9 Beat in the butter and icing sugar and blend until smooth. Pour the glaze over the cake. (If the glaze is too thick to pour, just put it back over the boiling water until it is of pouring consistency.)

Mini Carrot Cakes with Cream Cheese Icing

Makes approx. 5 dozen squares

When I did the show talking about my twentieth high-school reunion, it sounded more like a session with psychologist Norm Forman than a cooking time slot. Like anyone who has gone to a school reunion, I approached the event with nervous anticipation. I felt lucky in some ways, however, as I was in charge of the food and knew I could always hide in the kitchen!

One of the things we made were these mini carrot cakes—they're easy to eat, look great and taste delicious. As it turned out, people were almost too busy talking to one another to eat—a sign of a successful reunion to be sure!

You can freeze individual squares and just use as many as you need at a time. They are great to have on hand. Ice them with the cream cheese icing and decorate with toasted coconut, or make little marzipan carrots for the top. Just buy marzipan and mix batches with green and orange food colouring. Roll tiny carrot shapes with your fingers and top with green leaf shapes.

½ cup	chopped toasted walnuts	125 mL
⅓ cup	unsweetened grated coconut	75 mL
½ cup	raisins	125 mL
2	large carrots, grated	2
1¾ cups	all-purpose flour	425 mL
pinch	salt	pinch
1½ tsp	baking powder	7 mL
½ tsp	baking soda	2 mL
1½ tsp	cinnamon	7 mL
¼ tsp	nutmeg	1 mL
pinch	allspice	pinch
3	eggs	3
¾ cup	brown sugar	175 mL
½ cup	granulated sugar	125 mL
¾ cup	safflower or corn oil	175 mL
CREAM CHEESE ICING		
6 oz	cream cheese	175 g
¼ cup	unsalted butter	50 mL
1 tsp	pure vanilla extract	5 mL
3 cups	sifted icing sugar	750 mL

1. Preheat the oven to 325°F/160°C. Butter a large 12-in x 18-in/30-cm x 46-cm roasting pan and line with parchment paper.
2. Combine the walnuts, coconut, raisins and carrots. Reserve.
3. Sift together the flour, salt, baking powder, baking soda, cinnamon, nutmeg and allspice. Reserve.
4. Beat the eggs and gradually add the sugars. Slowly add the oil, beating constantly.

5 Add the dry ingredients to the egg mixture all at once. Blend in as quickly as possible. Stir in the nut-carrot mixture.

6 Pour the batter into the prepared pan and bake for 30 to 35 minutes or until the cake springs back when touched gently in the centre. Cool for 15 minutes and invert.

7 To make the icing, beat the cream cheese until smooth and light. Beat in the butter until well blended.

8 Blend in the vanilla. Add the icing sugar 1 cup/250 mL at a time and blend in until the icing is light and spreadable (you may need more or less of the icing sugar).

9 Ice the cake with the cream cheese icing and decorate with toasted coconut and/or marzipan carrots. Cut the cake into 2-in/5-cm squares and place each square in a foil cup.

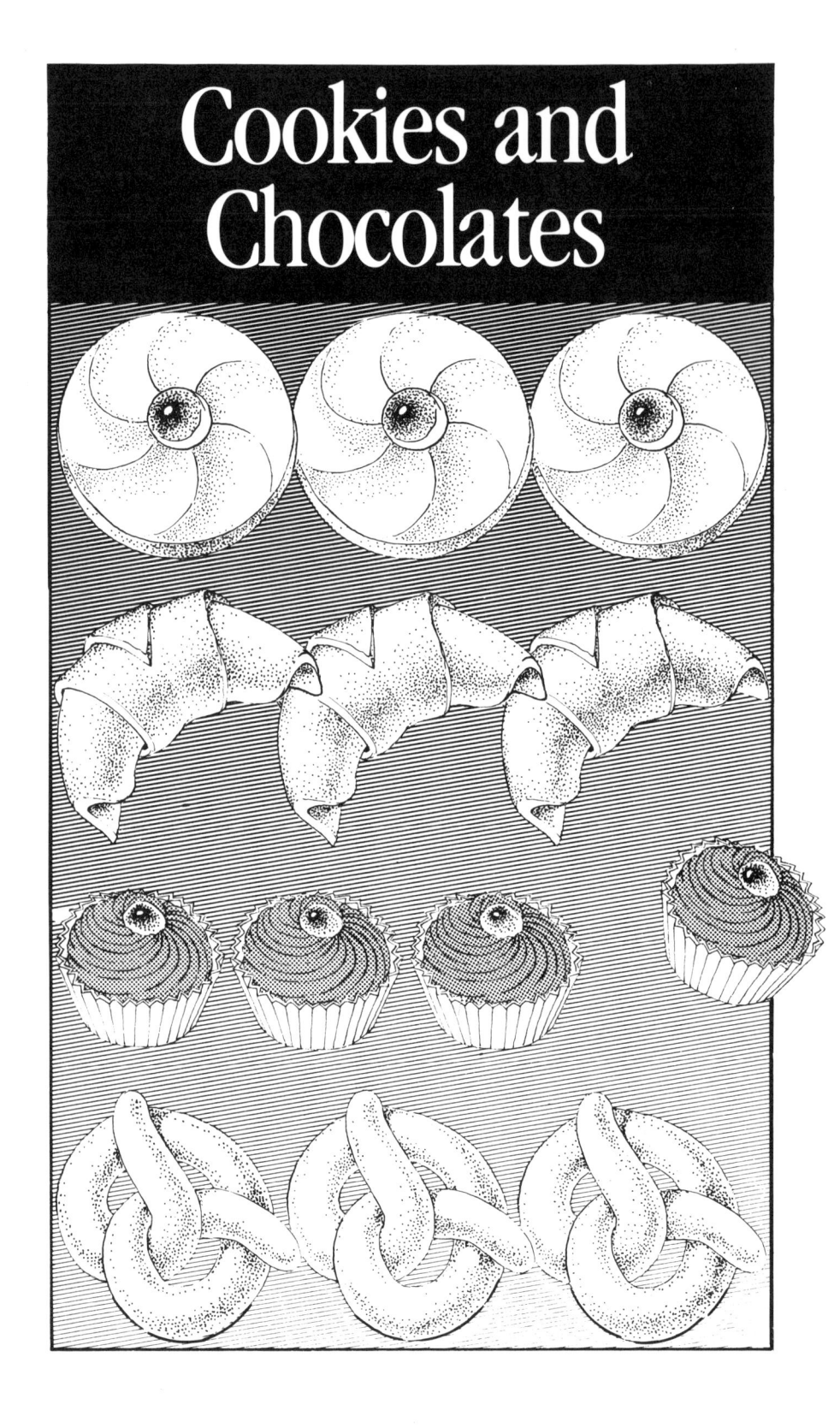

Cookies and Chocolates

COOKIES AND CHOCOLATES

The Shortest Shortbread

Makes approx. 7 dozen cookies

Whenever I want a favour from Brenda Burns, director of public relations and promotion at CKFM, all I have to do is make these cookies.

These are the cookies that we give out as special gifts at Christmas time. One year Sadie, the manager of my cookware shop, took one hundred boxes home in her car to deliver the next day. Thieves, spying these valuable-looking packages, broke into her car and started down the street with them. Neighbourhood Watch saved the day again and chased the thieves, whereupon the culprits dropped everything and ran. Fortunately, we only lost a few dozen in breakage, and we got to eat the broken cookies. After all, they're all the same once they're in your stomach!

If you can't find rice flour in your supermarket, try a health- or bulk-food store.

1 lb	salted butter*	500 g
1 cup	fruit sugar**	250 mL
3½ cups	all-purpose flour	875 mL
½ cup	rice flour	125 mL

1 Preheat the oven to 300°F/150°C. Butter the cookie sheets or line them with parchment paper.
2 Cream the butter until light. Gradually beat in the sugar.
3 Combine the flours and add to the butter-sugar mixture.
4 The dough can be patted into the cookie sheets, pricked with a fork, baked and then cut into pieces. Or it can be rolled out and cut with cookie cutters; or it can be formed into balls and pressed down with a fork, glass or potato masher for a more interesting design. Bake for 25 to 35 minutes until just barely golden.

* *I rarely use salted butter, but the flavour of these cookies depends on it.*
** *Fruit sugar can be made by processing 2 cups/500 mL regular granulated sugar in a blender or food processor for 60 to 90 seconds. Remeasure the sugar after processing (fruit sugar is also usually available at the supermarket).*

Soufflé Brownies

Makes 30 squares

This recipe for light, luscious chocolate squares was given to me by my good friend and great cook, Gwen Fargeon. These freeze beautifully. And because they do not contain flour, they are also perfect for Passover.

	4 oz	unsweetened chocolate	125 g
	½ cup	unsalted butter	125 mL
	1½ cups	fruit sugar* (see page 137)	375 mL
	4	eggs, separated	4
	¼ cup	finely chopped walnuts	50 mL
GARNISH	2 oz	semisweet or bittersweet chocolate	60 g
	30	walnut halves	30

1. Melt the chocolate in the top of a double boiler over barely simmering water. Cool.
2. Preheat the oven to 400°F/200°C. Butter a 9-in x 16-in/22-cm x 40-cm jelly roll pan, line it with parchment paper and butter again.
3. Cream the butter until light. Beat in the sugar gradually.
4. Beat in the melted chocolate. Add the egg yolks and combine well.
5. Beat the egg whites until stiff. Gently fold the egg whites into the chocolate base. Fold in the chopped walnuts.
6. Reserve and refrigerate ¾ cup/175 mL of this chocolate mixture. Spread the remaining mixture over the cookie sheet. Bake for 10 to 12 minutes until the top is firm but not too dry. Cool.
7. Trim the hard edges off the chocolate cake base (eat them). Divide the cake in half and gently remove it from the parchment paper.
8. Spread one half of the cake with the unbaked chocolate mixture. Top with the second baked half. Cut the cake into 30 squares.
9. For the garnish, melt the semisweet chocolate and place a dab on each square. Top with a walnut half and refrigerate.

Sarah Band's Lemon Squares

Makes 16 squares

Sarah Band was a Cordon Bleu caterer before she opened her fabulous shop, Sarahband, on Yorkville Avenue in Toronto. Her store is packed with stunning serving pieces, silver and all kinds of elegant tableware.

BASE	½ cup	unsalted butter	125 mL
	2 tbsp	brown sugar	25 mL
	1 cup	all-purpose flour	250 mL
	pinch	salt	pinch
FILLING	2	eggs	2
	1 cup	granulated sugar	250 mL
	2 tsp	all-purpose flour	10 mL
	1½ cups	dessicated coconut	375 mL
		Juice and finely grated peel of 1 lemon	
ICING	¼ cup	unsalted butter	50 mL
		Juice of 1 lemon	
	¾ cup	icing sugar (approximately)	175 mL

1 Preheat the oven to 350°F/180°C.

2 To make the base, cream ½ cup/125 mL butter with the brown sugar. Add 1 cup/250 mL flour and the salt. Press into the bottom of an 8-in/1.5-L buttered baking dish. Bake for 10 minutes.

3 To make the filling, combine the eggs with the granulated sugar, 2 tsp/10 mL flour, coconut, juice and peel of one lemon. Pour the filling over the base and bake for 20 minutes. Cool completely.

4 To make the icing, cream ¼ cup/50 mL butter and add the juice of one lemon. Add enough icing sugar to make a spreadable icing. Spread over the filling. Cut into 16 squares.

Chocolate Blizzard Cookies

Makes approx. 36 cookies*

These cookies are so rich and delicious that you have to hide them from yourself so you won't eat them all at once! The white chocolate "chips" inside are a wonderful change from regular dark chocolate chip cookies. But, of course, if you do not like change, just use bittersweet or semisweet chips and call these cookies Chocolate Tornado Cookies.

Peter Pacini, the executive producer of "Hour Toronto Magazine", has been known to propose to anyone who makes these cookies for him. But he is so erratic about it that his wife Margie and kids, Caleigh and Jamie, need not really worry.

1 lb	bittersweet or semisweet chocolate, chopped	500 g
¼ cup	unsalted butter	50 mL
½ cup	all-purpose flour	125 mL
½ tsp	baking powder	2 mL
¼ tsp	salt	1 mL
4	eggs	4
¾ cup	brown sugar	175 mL
¾ cup	granulated sugar	175 mL
10 oz	white chocolate, chopped	300 g
2 cups	chopped toasted pecans	500 mL

1. Melt the chocolate and butter over hot water. Cool slightly.
2. Sift together the flour, baking powder and salt. Reserve.
3. Beat the eggs with the sugars until light and stir in the melted chocolate. Add the flour mixture, chopped white chocolate and nuts. Refrigerate the dough until it is cold enough to mould.
4. Shape the dough into two flat rolls about 3 in/7.5 cm in diameter, like refrigerator cookies. Roll in additional flour and wrap well in waxed paper. (Don't worry about the floury edges of the cookies after they are baked. It makes them look more blizzardy!) Freeze for 1 hour.
5. Preheat the oven to 350°F/180°C. Line cookie sheets with parchment paper. Slice the cookies ½ in/1 cm thick. Bake only 10 to 12 minutes or just until they lose their sheen. They should just barely hold their shape when cool, and should be moist and chewy inside. Gently lift the cookies off the cookie sheets and cool on racks.

* *You don't have to bake these cookies all at once. They are very rich, so just cut off what you need for baking. They also freeze well after they are baked.*

Rugalahs (Cinnamon Crescents)

Makes 24 crescents

This is probably my students' all-time favourite recipe. People used to leave the class and head straight for the closest convenience store to buy the ingredients. If they could have made them in the car on the way home, they would have!

PASTRY	½ cup	unsalted butter, cold, cut into pieces	125 mL
	1 cup	all-purpose flour	250 mL
	4 oz	cream cheese, cold, cut into pieces	125 g
	½ cup	raspberry jam	125 mL
FILLING	¼ cup	brown sugar	50 mL
	⅓ cup	finely chopped walnuts	75 mL
	1 tbsp	cinnamon	15 mL
	1 tbsp	cocoa	15 mL
	1 tsp	finely grated orange peel (optional)	5 mL
GLAZE	1	egg	1
	2 tbsp	cream	25 mL
	⅓ cup	coarse white sugar or chopped nuts or regular sugar	75 mL

1. Make the pastry by cutting the butter into the flour until crumbly. Then cut in the cheese until crumbly. Gather the dough together and form a ball. Knead a few times. Divide dough in half and shape into two balls. Wrap and refrigerate until ready to use. (The pastry can be easily made in a food processor—process until the dough just comes together.)

2. Prepare the filling by combining the brown sugar, nuts, cinnamon, cocoa and orange peel.

3. Preheat the oven to 350°F/180°C.

4. Roll out each ball of dough into a circle. The thinner the pastry, the crisper the cookies will be. Spread each round with a thin layer of jam. Sprinkle with the filling and pat it in firmly.

5. Cut each circle into 12 wedges and roll each wedge up tightly from the outside edge, as shown.

6. Butter a cookie sheet well or line with parchment paper. Arrange the crescents on the cookie sheet. Combine the egg and cream. Brush the cookies with the glaze and sprinkle with sugar. (Crescents can now be frozen.)

7. Bake for 20 to 25 minutes until golden. (Frozen crescents will require a slightly longer baking time.)

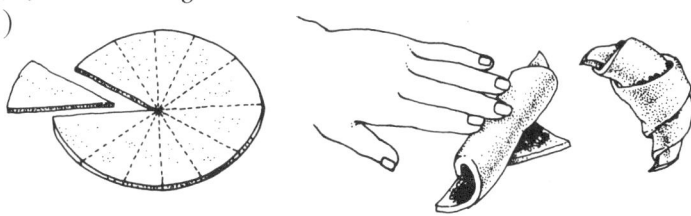

Chocolate Truffles with Grand Marnier

Makes approx. 4 dozen

It is easy to make your own truffles. These are what chocoholics' dreams are made of!
I always use the best-quality chocolate I can find. If you're going to gain weight, it should be on the best food possible! Even though Swiss chocolate sounds as if it should be more expensive than domestic, it rarely is, and the flavour and texture are far superior. It does not come premeasured for you, however, and therefore a set of scales comes in handy when using it. If you are using the large 370-g Swiss chocolate bars that have 40 small squares, three little squares equals one ounce.

12 oz	bittersweet or semisweet chocolate	375 g
½ cup	unsalted butter	125 mL
3	egg yolks	3
2 tbsp	Grand Marnier	25 mL
1 cup	cocoa, sifted	250 mL

1. Chop the chocolate and place in the top of a double boiler over barely simmering water. Add the butter and cook, stirring, until melted together.
2. Beat in the egg yolks and stir until smooth. Cook for 1 minute. Beat in the liqueur.
3. Transfer the mixture to a bowl. Cover. Refrigerate until firm.
4. Using a spoon or melon baller, shape the chocolate mixture into 1-in/2.5-cm balls. Roll in cocoa.

VARIATIONS

Almond Add ½ cup/125 mL ground toasted almonds to the chocolate mixture and use Amaretto instead of Grand Marnier. Roll the truffles in ground toasted almonds instead of cocoa.

Hazelnut Add ½ cup/125 mL ground toasted hazelnuts to the chocolate mixture and use Frangelico instead of Grand Marnier. Roll the truffles in ground toasted hazelnuts.

Mocha Use 1 tbsp/15 mL dark rum and 1 tbsp/15 mL coffee liqueur instead of Grand Marnier. Roll the truffles in sifted icing sugar.

Cognac Use Cognac instead of Grand Marnier. Roll in cocoa.

Raspberry Truffles

Makes approx. 6 dozen

Other liqueurs can be used in place of the raspberry liqueur, but raspberry and chocolate make a special combination. These freeze well (well wrapped) for a few months. They should only be kept in the refrigerator for up to one week.

12 oz	bittersweet chocolate	375 g
½ cup	whipping cream	125 mL
⅓ cup	unsalted butter	75 mL
½ cup	icing sugar, sifted	125 mL
4	egg yolks	4
¼ cup	Chambord or other raspberry liqueur or eau de vie	50 mL
½ cup	cocoa, sifted	125 mL
½ cup	icing sugar, sifted	125 mL
½ cup	finely chopped almonds or hazelnuts	125 mL

1. Melt the chocolate with the cream and butter over very low heat.
2. Stir in ½ cup/125 mL icing sugar and the egg yolks and beat until smooth.
3. Add the Chambord and refrigerate until firm.
4. Roll the chocolate into bite-sized balls. Roll one-third of the truffles in cocoa, one-third in ½ cup/125 mL icing sugar and one-third in nuts. Place in little paper cups and refrigerate or freeze. Serve chilled.

Hazelnut Chocolates

Makes approx. 4 dozen

This is a favourite of our students, especially for giving as Christmas gifts.

Bittersweet and semisweet chocolate can be used interchangeably. Bittersweet is a European term that usually refers to chocolate slightly less sweet than semisweet, and that's what I prefer to cook with. In fact, whenever a recipe calls for semisweet or sweet chocolate, I use bittersweet. And don't be misled by the word "bitter." It's absolutely fantastic for eating.

To toast hazelnuts, spread the nuts on a cookie sheet and bake at 350° F/180° C for 5 to 10 minutes until toasted. Gather the nuts in a tea towel and rub together until the skins flake off. You will never be able to rub off all the skins, so don't worry.

8 oz	bittersweet chocolate, melted	250 g
½ cup	unsalted butter	125 mL
½ cup	icing sugar, sifted	125 mL
3 tbsp	hazelnut liqueur (Frangelico)	50 mL
48	hazelnuts, lightly toasted with skins rubbed off	48

1. Cool the melted chocolate until still liquid but at room temperature.
2. Beat the butter until light and gradually beat in the sugar. Add the liqueur and then the chocolate. Beat well.
3. Place the chocolate mixture in a piping tube with a small star nozzle and pipe into tiny paper cups or onto parchment paper.
4. Top each chocolate with a toasted hazelnut. Chill.

Desserts and Pastries

Russian Mousse with Strawberry Sauce

Serves 6 to 8

This creamy concoction has the dairy flavour I adore. If you make it in a heart-shaped mould, it's a perfect dessert for Valentine's Day.

The sauce can also be made with frozen strawberries or raspberries. Use the individually quick frozen ones for best results.

RUSSIAN MOUSSE		
1	envelope unflavoured gelatine	1
¼ cup	water, cold	50 mL
3	egg yolks	3
⅓ cup	sugar	75 mL
1 cup	milk, hot	250 mL
1 tsp	pure vanilla extract	5 mL
1 cup	sour cream (preferably Astro)	250 mL
¾ cup	whipping cream	175 mL
STRAWBERRY SAUCE		
1 qt	strawberries	1 L
¼ cup	sugar	50 mL
¼ cup	Cointreau	50 mL

1. To make the mousse, sprinkle the gelatine over the water in a small saucepan. Allow it to soften for 5 minutes.
2. Beat the egg yolks with the sugar in a saucepan. Beat in the hot milk.
3. Heat the gelatine mixture gently and stir until dissolved. Stir it into the yolk mixture and cook over low heat until slightly thickened, about 5 minutes.
4. Stir in the vanilla and sour cream. Cool until the mixture reaches room temperature.
5. Beat the whipping cream until light and soft peaks form.
6. Fold the cream quickly into the sour cream base. Pour into a 3-cup/750-mL mould. Cover with plastic wrap and refrigerate for a few hours or overnight.
7. Save a few nice berries for the garnish. Puree the remaining berries with the sugar and Cointreau.
8. Before serving, run a knife around the outside of the mould and invert onto a serving plate. Slice into wedges. Serve with the sauce under or poured over the mousse. Garnish with the reserved berries.

DESSERTS AND PASTRIES

Maple Syrup Mousse

Serves 8

I love to promote Canadian cooking, and over the years various tour companies have hired me to do Canadian cooking demonstrations for visitors from other countries. This four-star Canadian dessert is one of the all-time favourites.

When the International Association of Cooking Professionals Convention was in Toronto, we took delegates out to Norman Jewison's maple syrup farm, where they enjoyed a wonderful feast. Norman Jewison does his share to promote Canadian food by selling his exclusive maple syrup all over Hollywood.

1	envelope unflavoured gelatine	1
¼ cup	water, cold	50 mL
1 cup	pure maple syrup	250 mL
3	egg yolks	3
1 tsp	pure vanilla extract	5 mL
2 tbsp	coffee liqueur, such as Tia Maria or Kahlua	25 mL
2½ cups	whipping cream	625 mL
GARNISH	Chocolate coffee beans or chocolate curls	

1 In a small saucepan, sprinkle the gelatine over the cold water and allow it to soften for about 5 minutes.
2 In a separate saucepan, bring the maple syrup to a boil.
3 Heat the gelatine mixture just until the gelatine dissolves.
4 Beat the egg yolks and slowly whisk in the hot maple syrup. Whisk in the gelatine mixture as well.
5 Return the egg-yolk mixture to the heat and cook gently over low heat until it turns slightly custardy, about 5 minutes. Remove from the heat and stir in the vanilla and liqueur. Cool to room temperature. (This can be done over a bowl of ice cubes, or place the mixture in the refrigerator for about 30 minutes.) Do not allow the gelatine to set. (If the gelatine does set, simply set it over a bowl of hot water until it becomes liquid again.)
6 Whip the cream until it is light and soft peaks form. Fold it gently into the maple base. Spoon the mousse into individual dessert dishes and top with chocolate coffee beans or chocolate curls. Chill for at least 1 hour before serving.

DESSERTS AND PASTRIES

Amaretto Trifle

Serves 6

Amaretto, an almond-flavoured liqueur made from apricot kernels, has become incredibly popular. This is a pretty dessert that can easily be made a day ahead. It can be prepared in a large bowl or individual glasses. Rum, Grand Marnier or other liqueurs can be used instead of Amaretto. But change the name!

CAKE	8 oz	sponge cake (see page 128)	250 g
	¼ cup	Amaretto	50 mL
	1 pint	strawberries	500 mL
	½ cup	sliced toasted almonds	125 mL
CUSTARD	¼ cup	cornstarch	50 mL
	⅓ cup	sugar	75 mL
	pinch	salt	pinch
	3 cups	milk, cold	750 mL
	4	egg yolks	4
	½ cup	cream	125 mL
	¼ cup	Amaretto	50 mL
	1 tsp	pure vanilla extract	5 mL
	¼ tsp	almond extract	1 mL
GARNISH	1 cup	whipping cream	250 mL
	2 tbsp	Amaretto	25 mL
		Reserved strawberries and almonds	

1. Cut the cake into small cubes and spread out in one layer on a cookie sheet or waxed paper. Sprinkle with ¼ cup/50 mL Amaretto.

2. Reserve the nicest 6 strawberries for a garnish. Slice the rest and reserve. Put aside 2 tbsp/25 mL almonds for the garnish as well.

3. To prepare the custard, combine the cornstarch, sugar and salt in a heavy saucepan. Whisk in ½ cup/125 mL cold milk and blend well. Then add the remaining milk. Cook the custard over gentle heat, stirring constantly, until thickened, about 5 minutes.

4. Combine the egg yolks with the cream. Add a little of the hot custard to the yolks to raise the temperature gradually, and then add the yolks to the custard. Cook for a few minutes longer.

5. Stir in ¼ cup/50 mL Amaretto, the vanilla and almond extract. Remove from the heat. Cover with buttered waxed paper to prevent a skin from forming and cool slightly.

6. Divide the cake, sliced strawberries and almonds among six brandy snifters, large wine glasses or dessert bowls. Pour an equal amount of custard over the cake in each glass.

7. To prepare the garnish, beat the whipping cream until stiff. Beat in 2 tbsp/25 mL Amaretto. Pipe or spoon the cream on top of each serving. Top with a whole strawberry and sprinkle with the reserved almonds.

Chocolate Mousse

Serves 4

There are so many chocolate mousse recipes. Try this one and you'll never have to decide again which one to choose!

	4 oz	semisweet or bittersweet chocolate	125 g
	¼ cup	unsalted butter	50 mL
	2 tbsp	orange liqueur (Cointreau, Grand Marnier or Triple Sec)	25 mL
	3	egg yolks	3
	½ tsp	pure vanilla extract	2 mL
	¾ cup	whipping cream	175 mL
GARNISH	¾ cup	whipping cream, whipped	175 mL
	¼ cup	chopped chocolate-coated candied orange peel (optional)	50 mL

1 Melt the chocolate in the top of a double boiler over hot but not boiling water.

2 Beat in the butter until it melts. Add the liqueur and egg yolks and beat thoroughly. Cook gently for a few minutes.

3 Stir in the vanilla. Cool until the chocolate comes to room temperature.

4 Beat ¾ cup/175 mL whipping cream until it is light and soft peaks form. Fold it into the cooled chocolate mixture. Pour the mousse into individual serving dishes and refrigerate for at least 3 hours.

5 Garnish the mousse with whipped cream and the chocolate-coated candied orange peel.

Coffee Crème Caramel

Serves 6 to 8

The world is divided between chocolate-lovers and caramel-lovers. I am definitely a caramel person.

Some recipes for caramel suggest melting the sugar alone, but I have found that using a little water with the sugar helps to control the crystallization and burning.

CARAMEL	1 cup	sugar	250 mL
	¼ cup	water	50 mL
CUSTARD	1 cup	milk	250 mL
	2 cups	cream	500 mL
	2 tbsp	coffee, ground for the percolator	25 mL
	2	whole eggs	2
	6	egg yolks	6
	⅓ cup	sugar	75 mL
	2 tsp	pure vanilla extract	10 mL

1 Preheat the oven to 350°F/180°C.

2 To prepare the caramel, place 1 cup/250 mL sugar and the water in a heavy saucepan and stir together well. Heat gently to dissolve the sugar, stirring, then turn up the heat and stop stirring.

3 Cook over high heat for 5 to 10 minutes, or until the caramel turns a golden colour. (Have a small bowl of water and a pastry brush on hand to brush sugar crystals down the sides of the pot.) Slowly pour into a 6-cup/1.5-L soufflé dish. (Make sure the dish you are pouring the hot caramel into is at room temperature. The caramel is very hot and could break a cold dish.) Swirl the caramel in the dish to coat the sides partway up. Reserve.

4 To make the custard, combine the milk, cream and coffee in a saucepan and heat. Cook gently for about 5 minutes. Strain through a coffee filter or paper towel-lined sieve.

5 Beat the eggs and egg yolks with ⅓ cup/75 mL sugar. Beat in the milk mixture. Add the vanilla. Strain the custard into the caramel-lined pan.

6 Bake the custard in a water bath (a larger pan partially filled with very hot water coming about halfway up the sides of the custard dish) for 40 to 50 minutes or until set. Cool, then refrigerate overnight.

7 To unmould, run a knife around the edge of the custard and invert carefully onto a dish that has a small lip, to prevent the caramel from leaking over. Serve in wedges with a spoonful of the runny caramel over the top. (You can serve this with whipped cream, but I like it the way it is.)

DESSERTS AND PASTRIES

Best Rice Pudding

Serves 4 to 6

This is "Hour Toronto Magazine's" favourite recipe. (This is the reason we request that listeners send in self-addressed envelopes. When this recipe was aired, 450 people called in one day for copies and it nearly broke the bank!) More people have asked for this recipe than any other, and it has been reported that it even saved a marriage! It sounds like a lot of liquid for a little rice, but when it has cooked enough it will be thick. Trust me.

Short-grain rice is used when you want the finished result to be creamy, so it is usually preferred in dessert recipes.

1 cup	water	250 mL
½ cup	short-grain rice	125 mL
5 cups	milk	1.25 L
½ cup	sugar	125 mL
1 tsp	cornstarch	5 mL
½ cup	raisins	125 mL
pinch	nutmeg	pinch
1	egg yolk	1
1 tsp	pure vanilla extract	5 mL
1 tbsp	cinnamon	15 mL
	Cream (optional)	

1. Bring the water and the rice to a boil in a large saucepan for 15 minutes or until the water is absorbed.
2. Stir 4½ cups/1.125 L milk into the rice and heat gently.
3. Combine the sugar and cornstarch and stir in the remaining ½ cup/125 mL milk. Stir into the rice mixture. Add the raisins and nutmeg.
4. Stirring constantly, bring this to a gentle boil. Reduce the heat to low and cover. Simmer gently for 1 to 1½ hours or until the pudding has thickened, stirring occasionally. (The time will vary according to the stove and the pot.)
5. When the pudding is thick, add a little to the egg yolk, then beat the yolk into the pudding. Cook gently for another 2 minutes. Remove from the heat and add the vanilla.
6. Spoon the pudding into serving bowls and sprinkle cinnamon over the top. Serve with cream if you are thin. This is good hot or cold, so try it both ways. (The pudding gets even thicker when it cools.)

Frozen Grand Marnier Soufflé with Hot Chocolate Sauce

Serves 12

Many people think you need an ice-cream machine to make homemade ice cream. But this frozen dessert can be made perfectly, even without one.

GRAND MARNIER SOUFFLÉ

1 cup	granulated sugar	250 mL
½ cup	water	125 mL
6	egg yolks	6
¼ cup	icing sugar	50 mL
2 tsp	pure vanilla extract	10 mL
½ cup	Grand Marnier or other orange liqueur	125 mL
3 cups	whipping cream	750 mL

HOT CHOCOLATE SAUCE

8 oz	semisweet or bittersweet chocolate	250 g
1 cup	whipping cream	250 mL
2 tbsp	Grand Marnier	25 mL

1. Combine the granulated sugar and water together in a heavy saucepan. Cook, stirring, until the mixture comes to a boil. Continue to cook, without stirring, until the mixture reaches 240°F/115°C on a candy thermometer (and is at the soft ball stage when a bit of the syrup is dropped into a glass of cold water—about 5 to 7 minutes).

2. Meanwhile, beat the egg yolks with the icing sugar until light and fluffy (use a mixmaster or hand mixer for the best results).

3. Slowly drip the sugar syrup into the egg-yolk mixture, beating constantly. Continue to beat the mixture until it is completely cool and very light.

4. Stir in the vanilla and ½ cup/125 mL Grand Marnier.

5. Whip the cream until it is light and forms soft peaks. Gently fold into the Grand Marnier base. Pour the mixture into a 10-in/25-cm springform pan and cover with plastic wrap. Freeze immediately. When frozen, wrap well if you are planning to keep it for longer than two days.

6. To make the sauce, melt the chocolate and the cream in the top of a double boiler. Beat well until combined thoroughly.

7. Stir in 2 tbsp/25 mL Grand Marnier and serve hot. (The sauce may be prepared ahead, but it will solidify when refrigerated, so warm it again before serving.)

8. Before serving, place the frozen soufflé (if frozen solid) in the refrigerator for 30 minutes to make slicing easier. Run a knife around the inside edge of the springform pan and then unsnap the pan. Serve in wedges and pass the chocolate sauce separately.

DESSERTS AND PASTRIES

Raspberry Yogurt Mousse

Serves 8 to 10

Raspberries are an all-time favourite because of their distinctive sweet-tart taste. Fresh berries are so expensive that although you can use them in this dessert, it's almost best to reserve them for eating on their own. Individually quick frozen berries are a welcome addition to frozen food and can almost always be used interchangeably with fresh.

This recipe can also be halved.

	2	envelopes unflavoured gelatine	2
	⅓ cup	water, cold	75 mL
	2½ cups	raspberries, fresh or individually quick frozen, pureed*	
	½ cup	sugar	125 mL
	2 tbsp	lemon juice	25 mL
	2 tbsp	rum	25 mL
	1 cup	unflavoured yogurt (preferably Astro Balkan style)	250 mL
	2 cups	whipping cream	500 mL
GARNISH	10	fresh raspberries or fresh strawberries	10

1. Sprinkle the gelatine over the water in a medium-sized heavy saucepan. Allow it to soften for 5 minutes. Then heat gently and stir to dissolve.

2. In another saucepan, stir together the raspberry puree, sugar, lemon juice and rum. Heat just until the sugar has dissolved, about 5 minutes.

3. Whisk the raspberry puree into the dissolved gelatine. Cool for 10 minutes.

4. Combine the puree with the yogurt thoroughly. (If the mixture is not at room temperature, cool for a few minutes longer.)

5. Whip the cream until it is light and soft peaks form. Fold into the puree. Turn into a large glass serving bowl or individual dessert bowls. Allow to set for 2 hours for individual servings or 4 hours for a large bowl. Garnish with whole berries.

* *If you puree the berries in a food mill, it will also strain out the seeds. If you puree them in a blender or food processor and you do not want the seeds, simply strain the puree. You should have approximately 2 cups/500 mL puree.*

Coffee Ice Cream with Caramel Sauce

Serves 4 to 6

Although this sounds simple, the flavour combination is complex and heavenly. The caramel sauce is also great over bananas, in banana splits or anywhere a caramel sauce is called for. Always prepare caramel cautiously—it should be treated with respect. The best caramel is dark brown, but it burns easily, and if that happens it should be discarded. If you use an enamelled pan it is easier to see the colour of the caramel, but as long as the pan is heavy-bottomed, the recipe should work well.

¼ cup	water	50 mL
1 cup	sugar	250 mL
1 cup	whipping cream	250 mL
2 tbsp	unsalted butter	25 mL
1 pint	best-quality coffee ice cream (either homemade or Haägen Dazs)	500 mL

1. Combine the water and sugar in a 3-qt/3-L heavy saucepan. Cook over medium-high heat, stirring, until the sugar dissolves. Continue to cook, but do not stir. Cook until the sugar turns a golden caramel colour. (During the cooking, brush any sugar crystals down the sides of the pan with a pastry brush dipped in cold water.) Do not burn! (If the sugar crystallizes before browning, either add a little more water and cook until it melts, or start again and be careful not to stir after the sugar dissolves.)

2. Remove the pan from the heat and carefully add the cream. Stand back—the mixture will bubble up quite a bit and then settle down, so do not worry. Stir until smooth. (Return to the heat for a minute if necessary to smooth it.)

3. Add the butter and stir to melt. Allow to cool. Serve the sauce with the coffee ice cream. (The sauce can be served warm, at room temperature or cold. As it cools, the sauce will thicken. Store it in the refrigerator.)

Bread Pudding

Serves 8

There are probably as many bread pudding recipes as there are cooks who make it. With the popularity of regional North American cooking and Cajun cooking, it is enjoying quite a revival. Bread pudding is now served in some of the most prestigious restaurants in North America. Chopped pecans, grated coconut, candied fruit or grated chocolate can also be added to this recipe. You can add some or all of these—use about ½ cup/125 mL of each.

½ cup	unsalted butter, soft	125 mL
12	slices bread (preferably brioche or egg bread, crusts on or off)	12
½ cup	raisins or chopped dried apricots	125 mL
⅓ cup	brown sugar	75 mL
1 tbsp	cinnamon	15 mL
¼ tsp	nutmeg	1 mL
6	eggs	6
2	egg yolks	2
⅓ cup	granulated sugar	75 mL
3 cups	milk	750 mL
1 cup	cream	250 mL
1 tsp	pure vanilla extract	5 mL
½ cup	apricot jam	125 mL

1. Butter the bread on both sides. Line the bottom of a 3-qt/3-L casserole dish or oblong baking pan with some of the bread.

2. Combine the raisins, brown sugar, cinnamon and nutmeg. Sprinkle the bread with some of the mixture. Repeat the layers of bread and raisins until everything is used. Top with a layer of bread to prevent the raisins from burning.

3. Beat the eggs and egg yolks with the granulated sugar. Beat in the milk, cream and vanilla. Pour over the bread and allow to stand for 30 minutes until the bread has absorbed the custard.

4. Preheat the oven to 350°F/180°C. Bake the pudding for 30 minutes. Check, and if the pudding is browning too much, cover it loosely. Bake for 20 to 30 minutes longer or until puffed and browned.

5. Heat the apricot jam. Brush it on top of the pudding. Serve warm or cold.

Caramelized Applesauce

Makes approx. 3 cups/750 mL

I love caramel. My husband, Ray, loves apples. This combination is very delicious and pleases us both.

You can serve it over ice cream, as a crêpe filling, or as a condiment with goose, duck, roast pork or sausages. Or add ½ cup/125 mL whipping cream, reduce the sauce until thickened and use it as a sauce over chicken or pork. Or you can puree the sauce, fold in 1 cup/250 mL whipping cream, whipped, and serve it as an apple mousse.

10	apples (Golden Delicious, Spy or Ida Reds)	10
¼ cup	unsalted butter	50 mL
⅔ cup	sugar	150 mL

1 Peel the apples. Cut them in half and remove the cores. Slice them into slices about ½ in/1 cm thick.

2 Melt the butter in a large skillet and add the sugar. Cook for approximately 5 minutes. The sugar should begin to melt and turn golden. (Be careful not to burn it.)

3 Add the apples. At first the juices from the apples will come out but eventually, in about 20 minutes, the juices will evaporate and the mixture will start to thicken. The heat should be medium to medium-high. Cook for another 10 minutes until apples start to brown and stick—watch them closely and make sure they do not burn. Puree the apples to make a sauce or serve as is.

DESSERTS AND PASTRIES

Peach Flambé

Serves 6

Everyone makes a big deal about flambés, but there's really nothing to it. Flambés are done for three reasons—to burn off the alcohol, to singe the top of food (rather like a very quick broil), and for show. In any recipe, if your flambé does not ignite, don't worry. As soon as the mixture is brought to a boil, the alcohol will evaporate anyway. (You want the alcohol to evaporate because raw alcohol can give a slightly bitter taste.) If your flambé doesn't work the first time, try again, but stop there—you can over-liqueur a dish as easily as you can over-salt it. (If you plan to flambé, be sure to turn off any smoke detectors.)

This is a dessert I learned to make when I took my chef training almost twenty years ago (can that be right?). And I still love it! This recipe is also delicious made with pineapple or pears.

6	peach halves, poached or canned, with the juices	6
½ cup	sugar	125 mL
¼ cup	unsalted butter	50 mL
¼ cup	reserved peach juices (or apricot nectar)	50 mL
¼ cup	orange juice	50 mL
2 tbsp	lemon juice	25 mL
1	cinnamon stick, broken in two	1
4	whole cloves	4
1 tbsp	grated orange peel	15 mL
1 tbsp	grated lemon peel	15 mL
¼ cup	orange liqueur (such as Cointreau)	50 mL
⅓ cup	whipping cream	75 mL
2 tbsp	Cognac	25 mL

1 Drain the peach halves and reserve ¼ cup/50 mL of the juices.
2 Place the sugar in large heavy skillet. Heat until the sugar begins to melt and turn golden. Be careful not to burn it.
3 Add the butter and stir until it has melted. Do not worry if mixture is a bit lumpy at first.
4 Add all the fruit juices, cinnamon stick, cloves and peels. Cook for a few minutes.
5 Add the liqueur and the cream and cook a few minutes longer. Remove the cinnamon and cloves. Add the peaches but cook only until they are heated through.
6 Add the Cognac. Ignite. The idea is to catch the alcohol just as it is evaporating off the surface of the dish. If you are not sure about that precise moment, simply use a long fireplace match and wait for it to ignite. Serve with caramel or vanilla ice cream.

Deep-dish Apple, Pear and Apricot Pie

Serves 8

I don't often mention restaurants on the air, and when I do, I'm always afraid that Jeremy Brown, who eats out a lot, won't like the ones I pick. But with Trappers, a new restaurant in Toronto, we agreed whole-heartedly. They serve this outstanding pie. Chris Boland, the owner, was kind enough to share the recipe with "Hour Toronto Magazine" listeners. It is great served with ice cream.

FILLING	6	large Spy apples	6
	1	large Bartlett pear	1
	½ cup	dried apricots	125 mL
	2 tsp	lemon juice	10 mL
	⅓ cup	sugar	75 mL
	2 tbsp	cornstarch	25 mL
	1 tsp	cinnamon	5 mL
	pinch	nutmeg	pinch
PASTRY	1½ cups	all-purpose flour	375 mL
	pinch	salt	pinch
	⅓ cup	lard, cold, cut into bits	75 mL
	¼ cup	unsalted butter, cold, cut into bits	50 mL
	1	egg	1
	¼ cup	water, cold	50 mL

1 Preheat the oven to 400°F/200°C.

2 To make the filling, peel, core and slice the apples and pear. Chop the apricots coarsely (scissors work well).

3 Mix the fruits together and then toss with the lemon juice, sugar, cornstarch, cinnamon and nutmeg. Arrange in a 9-in x 13-in/3-L casserole or baking dish (approximately 3 in/7 cm deep).

4 To make the pastry, combine the flour with the salt. Cut in the lard and butter until they are in tiny pieces.

5 Beat the egg with the water and sprinkle enough over the pastry until you can gather the dough into a ball. Reserve the remaining egg mixture.

6 Roll out the dough to fit the top of the baking dish. Fit the pastry over the fruit mixture. Brush the top with remaining egg wash and prick the dough with a fork.

7 Bake for 50 to 60 minutes. If the top browns too much, reduce the heat for the last 20 minutes of the baking time. Serve warm.

DESSERTS AND PASTRIES

Fresh Peach Pie

Makes one 10-in/25-cm pie

All cooks have their preferences about what kind of fat to use in pastry. Butter has a wonderful flavour, gives an incredible aroma, and colours the crust beautifully. But lard (an animal fat) and shortening (a vegetable fat) are easier to work with and give a very flaky texture. If I'm serving a pastry hot (such as a quiche) I usually use a combination of butter and lard. But if a dessert is to be served at room or cold temperature, then I usually use all butter. Even though it may be a little heavier and a little more difficult to handle, the flavour and feel is better.

CRUST	⅔ cup	unsalted butter, cold, cut into bits	150 mL
	2 cups	all-purpose flour	500 mL
	¼ cup	ice water, or more if necessary	50 mL
FILLING	5 cups	sliced fresh peaches*	1.25 L
	½ cup	brown sugar	125 mL
	½ cup	all-purpose flour	125 mL
	1 tsp	cinnamon	5 mL
TOPPING	1	egg	1
	1 tbsp	cream	15 mL
	1 tbsp	granulated sugar (preferably coarse)	15 mL

1 Preheat the oven to 425°F/220°C.
2 Cut the butter into the flour until the butter is in tiny pieces. Sprinkle with water and gather the dough together into a ball. Use more water only if necessary. Divide the dough in half, with one piece slightly larger than the other.
3 Roll out the larger piece of dough and fit it into a 10-in/25-cm pie dish.
4 Combine all the ingredients for the filling and place in the pastry-lined dish.
5 Roll out the smaller piece of dough and cut it into strips. Fit the strips across the filling. (For an easy, attractive lattice design, see below.) Crimp the edges.
6 Combine the beaten egg with the cream. Brush the top strips and border of the pie with the glaze. Sprinkle with granulated sugar. Place the pie on a jellyroll pan.
7 Bake for 15 minutes. Reduce the heat to 350°F/180°C and bake for another 40 minutes.

* *To peel peaches easily, place them in boiling water for 1 minute. Rinse with cold water and peel. After peeling, pitting and slicing, drain the peaches well before adding them to the flour and sugar.*

Blueberry Lemon Mousse Pie

Makes one 10-in/25-cm pie

Many people think that there's a big secret to making pastry. My students will often tell me about a great-aunt who has been making pastry for fifty years and has a secret trick of only using lard. Or a grandmother who has been making pastry for seventy-five years and always uses a little bit of lemon juice in the water. But the real secret is that these people have been making pastry for a long time. As I always tell Judy Webb, who has a pastry phobia, if you only make pastry once a year, you will never get any better. But if you make pastry once a week for even a few months, you will soon be an expert!

This is a rich pastry that uses all butter. It has a wonderful flavour but is very delicate. If it breaks as you're rolling it, do not reroll. Simply lift in sections and pat into the pie dish, pressing the edges together.

CRUST	1½ cups	all-purpose flour	375 mL
	pinch	salt	pinch
	¾ cup	unsalted butter	175 mL
	2 tbsp	cold vinegar or lemon juice	25 mL
FILLING	1	envelope unflavoured gelatine	1
	¼ cup	water, cold	50 mL
	3	egg yolks	3
	¾ cup	granulated sugar	175 mL
	¾ cup	lemon juice	175 mL
	1 tbsp	grated lemon peel	15 mL
	1½ cups	whipping cream	375 mL
	2 cups	blueberries (preferably fresh)	500 mL
GARNISH	½ cup	whipping cream	125 mL
	2 tbsp	rum	25 mL
	2 tbsp	icing sugar	25 mL
	1 cup	blueberries	250 mL
	1	lemon, thinly sliced	1

1 To prepare the pastry, combine the flour with the salt and cut in the butter until it is in tiny pieces. Add the vinegar and gather the dough together to form a ball. Refrigerate for at least 30 minutes.

2 Preheat the oven to 425°F/220°C. Roll out the dough to fit a 10-in/25-cm pie dish and fit into the pan. Flute the edges. To bake blind, line the dough with parchment paper and fill with pie weights, raw rice or dried beans. Bake for 15 minutes. Remove the rice and paper, etc., and return to a 350°F/180°C oven for 10 to 15 minutes to cook through. Watch carefully. Cool thoroughly.

3 To make the filling, sprinkle the gelatine over the cold water in a saucepan. Allow it to rest for 5 minutes. Heat very gently until the gelatine has dissolved.

4 Beat the egg yolks with the granulated sugar until light and lemon-coloured. Beat in the lemon juice and peel.
5 Transfer the mixture to a saucepan and cook until the mixture thickens slightly, about 5 minutes. Stir in the dissolved gelatine. Remove from the heat, transfer the mixture to a bowl and cool until it is at room temperature but not yet set.
6 Beat 1½ cups/375 mL cream until it is light and soft peaks form. Then fold into the cooled lemon mousse.
7 Line the pastry with 2 cups/500 mL blueberries and spread the lemon mousse over the top. Refrigerate for 2 to 3 hours or until set.
8 Beat ½ cup/125 mL cream with the rum and icing sugar until stiff. Pipe or spoon attractively over the top of the pie. Garnish with blueberries and lemon slices.

Rhubarb Crisp

Serves 8

I don't think you can beat a rhubarb crisp for a great spring dessert. Serve it with ice cream or unwhipped whipping cream.

2 lb	**rhubarb, trimmed and sliced**	1 kg
2 tbsp	**unsalted butter, cut into bits**	25 mL
¼ cup	**granulated sugar**	50 mL
¾ cup	**all-purpose flour**	175 mL
½ cup	**rolled oats**	125 mL
½ cup	**brown sugar**	125 mL
½ cup	**granulated sugar**	125 mL
1 tsp	**cinnamon**	5 mL
½ cup	**unsalted butter**	125 mL

1 Preheat the oven to 375°F/190°C.
2 Combine the rhubarb, 2 tbsp/25 mL butter and ¼ cup/50 mL granulated sugar and place in a buttered 9-in x 13-in/3-L casserole dish.
3 Combine the flour, rolled oats, brown sugar, ½ cup/125 mL granulated sugar and cinnamon. Cut in ½ cup/125 mL butter until it is in tiny bits. Spread over the rhubarb.
4 Bake for 30 to 40 minutes or until the rhubarb is tender and the topping is crisp.

Fresh Fruit Tarts

Makes 24 2-in/5-cm tarts

When Judy Webb says she has problems with pastry, I can really sympathize. I always remember my mother making pastry from scratch for me when I was a child, and buying it frozen after my sister, Jani, was born. My mother used to say she couldn't be bothered to make pastry when she could buy it frozen. I therefore grew up thinking that pastry was a bother, which always makes a technique harder to master. I also grew up thinking that perhaps Mum loved me more because she made pastry from scratch for me. When questioned about this, my mother replied, "The truth of the matter is that I would have bought frozen pastry when you were little, too, but it wasn't available."

Although homemade pastry does require a little more work, it is worth the bother.

PASTRY	1½ cups	all-purpose flour	375 mL
	2 tbsp	sugar	25 mL
	¼ tsp	salt	1 mL
	½ cup	unsalted butter, cold	125 mL
	3 tbsp	ice water (or more)	50 mL
FILLING	2 oz	chocolate, melted or ½ cup/ 125 mL apricot or raspberry jam	60 g
	3 cups	fresh strawberries, blueberries, raspberries, blackberries, etc.	750 mL
GLAZE	1½ cups	apricot or raspberry jelly	375 mL

1. For the pastry, combine the flour with the sugar and salt. Cut in the butter until it is in tiny bits. Sprinkle with cold water and gather the dough together into a ball. Add more water by the spoonful if necessary to make a dough that is easy to handle but not too moist. Divide the dough in half, shape into balls and refrigerate in a plastic bag. Chill for 30 minutes.

2. Preheat the oven to 425°F/220°C. Roll out the dough into a thin circle about ⅛ in/ 3 mm thick. Cut with a 2½-in/6-cm round cookie cutter and fit the circles into the tart pans. Repeat with the remaining dough. Gather the remaining scraps and refrigerate for 10 minutes before re-rolling.

3. To bake the tart shells blind, place a paper muffin cup in each tart and weigh down with dry beans, uncooked rice or pie weights. (This will set the shape of the tarts and prevent bubbling.) Bake for 4 to 7 minutes. Remove the weights and paper. Lower the oven temperature to 350°F/180°C and bake for 7 to 10 minutes more until the pastry is browned and cooked through. Cool thoroughly.

4. Brush the bottom of the pastry with melted chocolate or jam. Fill with fruit.

5. Heat the jelly. If it is too thick to use as a glaze, simply thin with a little liqueur. Brush the top of the fruit with the glaze.

Butter Tarts

Makes 18 2-in/5-cm tarts

Although cookbooks often scare pastry makers with their neurotic warnings about over-handling the dough, usually it is okay unless you reroll. If you roll out your pastry and it looks like Norway with the fjords hanging off the sides, don't reroll. It only gets worse, never better.

Making little tarts, however, presents its own problems. You almost have to reroll the scraps to get the right number of tarts. After cutting out the first series of circles, rather than kneading the dough back together into a ball, I gingerly press the scraps together and roll. I rarely reroll the scraps more than once.

PASTRY	1½ cups	all-purpose flour	375 mL
	½ tsp	salt	2 mL
	½ cup	unsalted butter, cold	125 mL
	¼ cup	water, cold (or more if necessary)	50 mL
FILLING	¼ cup	unsalted butter	50 mL
	½ cup	brown sugar	125 mL
	1 cup	corn syrup	250 mL
	2	eggs	2
	1 tsp	pure vanilla extract	5 mL
	⅓ cup	raisins	75 mL
	⅓ cup	chopped walnuts	75 mL

1. Preheat the oven to 375°F/190°C.
2. To make the pastry, combine the flour and salt. Cut ½ cup/125 mL butter into the flour mixture and sprinkle with the water. Gather the dough together into a ball. Roll out and cut into 2½-in/6-cm circles. Fit the circles into the tart pans.
3. Blend together the ingredients for the filling, except for the raisins and nuts. Transfer the filling to a measuring cup or container with a spout.
4. Place a few raisins and nuts in each pastry-lined tart. Pour in the filling. Bake for 20 to 25 minutes. Cool thoroughly before removing from pans.

Especially for Kids

Yogurt Pancakes

Makes approx. 20

To say that my son is a picky eater is an understatement. But when Mark cooks with me, there is sometimes a chance that he will eat what he has helped prepare. So, obviously, I let him cook a lot. He loves to break the eggs for these pancakes. (My daughter, Anna, on the other hand, throws eggs all over the place.)

They both adore these pancakes, and when we make them in fancy shapes, and I let them put chocolate chips on them, they love them even more. To pipe them into the pan in fancy shapes, you can use a plastic ketchup or mustard container, though once when I was desperate and couldn't find the container (it was in the bathtub), I used a plastic baby bottle and an old nipple that I cut to enlarge the hole.

2	**eggs**	2
1½ cups	**unflavoured yogurt (preferably Astro)**	375 mL
2 tbsp	**sugar (optional)**	25 mL
¼ tsp	**salt (optional)**	1 mL
1 cup	**all-purpose flour**	250 mL
1 tsp	**baking soda**	5 mL
¼ cup	**unsalted butter**	50 mL
	Chocolate chips (optional)	
	Raisins (optional)	
	Fresh blueberries (optional)	

1. Break the eggs into a bowl and add the yogurt. Stir with a whisk. Stir in the sugar and salt if you are using them.

2. Sift the flour and baking soda into the egg mixture. Stir just until ingredients are mixed.

3. Melt the butter in a large skillet and pour it into the batter carefully. Mix in.

4. Return the pan to the heat. The pancakes can be made into rounds by dropping spoonfuls of batter into the pan. Happy faces or designs can be made with chocolate chips, raisins or blueberries. Numbers, letters, fish or boats can be made by pouring batter into a plastic ketchup bottle and writing with the batter directly in the pan.

5. Cook pancakes for about 2 minutes or until tiny bubbles appear and the surface has lost its sheen. Flip and cook the second side briefly. (Turn the letters and numbers over again before serving so they will be going in the right direction!) Serve with maple syrup, jam or corn syrup.

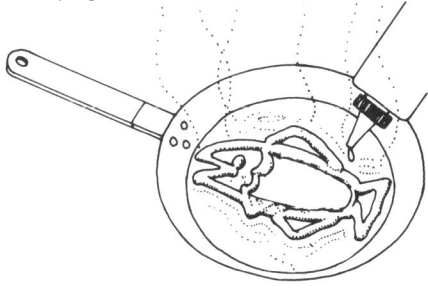

Caramel Corn

Makes 8 cups/2 L

I really love popcorn, and I really love caramel. Guess who could eat this whole recipe herself? This is great to give as party favours and terrific as a Halloween treat (though for actual trick-or-treating, I like to give prewrapped commercial candy).

Although this recipe is too difficult for younger children to make, they sure love to eat it. (Check with your pediatrician—some doctors caution against very young children eating popcorn.)

1 cup	packed brown sugar	250 mL
½ cup	unsalted butter	125 mL
¼ cup	corn syrup	50 mL
½ tsp	baking soda	2 mL
1 tbsp	pure vanilla extract	15 mL
8 cups	popped popcorn*	2 L

1. Preheat the oven to 275°F/135°C.
2. In a large pot, combine the sugar, butter and corn syrup. Boil for 2 minutes, stirring continuously. Remove from the heat.
3. Add the baking soda and vanilla. Combine the syrup with the popcorn and spread on a jelly roll pan.
4. Bake for 40 minutes, stirring every 10 minutes. Cool.

* *For 8 cups/2 L popped popcorn, use approximately ⅓ cup/75 mL unpopped popcorn.*

ESPECIALLY FOR KIDS

Easy Chocolate Mousse

Serves 6

This almost sounds too easy to be so delicious. (Sometimes I make this for a fast "gourmet" grown-up dessert and use bittersweet chocolate and 2 tbsp/25 mL Grand Marnier or Cognac.)

1 cup	chocolate chips (6 oz/175 g)	250 mL
1½ cups	whipping cream	375 mL
	Whole strawberries	

1. Place the chocolate chips in a bowl.
2. Heat 1 cup/250 mL cream and pour over the chips. Allow to stand for 30 seconds. Stir until the chocolate chips are melted and the mixture is smooth. Stir in the remaining cream.
3. Place the bowl in the refrigerator until the mixture is cold, about 30 minutes. (If you are in a hurry, place some ice and water in a large bowl and put the bowl of chocolate cream inside. This way it will chill in about 5 to 10 minutes.)
4. Beat the mixture with a hand mixer until whipped. Be careful not to overheat. Place in bowls and garnish with strawberries. Refrigerate for about 1 hour to firm or eat immediately if you do not mind it soft and creamy.

Wacky Cake

Serves 6 to 8

This is still one of the wackiest cakes I have ever seen! But it is great for kids to make—all in the same pan with hardly any utensils (I can't understand how they still manage to make a big mess).

My sister, Jani, is a grade three teacher and has always made a point of doing cooking projects with her students. Now that she's at home, she cooks with her kids, Charles and Meredith. When Meredith, age 4, is cooking and she is asked, "Who do you think you are?", she always replies Bonnie Stern.

1½ cups	all-purpose flour	375 mL
1 tsp	baking soda	5 mL
1 tsp	baking powder	5 mL
3 tbsp	cocoa	50 mL
1 cup	sugar	250 mL
1 tsp	cinnamon (optional)	5 mL
1 cup	milk	250 mL
⅓ cup	vegetable oil	75 mL
1 tbsp	white vinegar	15 mL
1 tsp	pure vanilla extract	5 mL
12	After Eight mints or 4 48-g Pep patties, broken into pieces	12

1. Preheat the oven to 350°F/180°C.
2. Place the dry ingredients in an 8-in/1.5-L square baking dish.
3. Combine the liquid ingredients in a large measuring cup and pour on top of the dry ingredients. Bake for 30 minutes.
4. Arrange the chocolate mint patties on top of the cake and return to the oven for 3 minutes. Swirl the chocolate over the top of the cake. Cool.

ESPECIALLY FOR KIDS

Mini Banana Muffins

Makes 36 mini muffins

Kids love these adorable little muffins, and they are great to take to children's programs when it's your turn to make the snack. They are so easy that the kids can help make them. And they freeze well so you can just defrost what you need at a time.

Use the mini muffin tins or even just aluminum foil cups that are approximately 1½-in/4 cm in diameter. To get the batter into the pans, kids love to use the mini ice-cream scoops!

For a more sophisticated dessert, hollow out the centre of the muffins with a melon baller, and pipe chocolate icing (see page 132) or partially set chocolate mousse (see page 149 or 167) into the hollows. Top with a banana chip.

2 cups	all-purpose flour	500 mL
¼ tsp	salt	1 mL
2 tsp	baking powder	10 mL
¼ tsp	baking soda	1 mL
½ cup	sugar	125 mL
⅓ cup	unsalted butter, melted	75 mL
1	small ripe banana, mashed	1
½ tsp	pure vanilla extract	2 mL
2	eggs	2
1 cup	unflavoured yogurt (preferably Astro)	250 mL
½ cup	chocolate chips (optional)	125 mL

1 Preheat the oven to 400°F/200°C. Butter 36 mini muffin cups or use mini foil cups.

2 Combine the dry ingredients together in a bowl.

3 Combine the melted butter with the mashed banana, vanilla, eggs and yogurt.

4 Pour the wet ingredients on top of the dry ingredients and combine only until mixed. Stir in the chocolate chips if you are using them.

5 Spoon the batter into the pans and bake for 10 to 15 minutes.

ESPECIALLY FOR KIDS

Chocolate Chip Oatmeal Cookies

Makes 4 dozen

As with all chocolate chip cookie batters, this one is delicious unbaked as well as baked. As a child I remember eating more unbaked, in fact. If you want them chewy, do not bake them too long. If you want them crisp, bake a little longer. (The first batch is usually experimental.)

¾ cup	unsalted butter	175 mL
1¼ cups	brown sugar	300 mL
1	egg	1
¼ cup	orange juice	50 mL
1 tsp	pure vanilla extract	5 mL
½ tsp	salt	2 mL
¼ tsp	baking soda	1 mL
1 cup	all-purpose flour	250 mL
3 cups	rolled oats	750 mL
1 cup	chocolate chips	250 mL

1. Preheat the oven to 350°F/180°C. Butter the cookie sheets or line with parchment paper.
2. Cream the butter until light. Gradually beat in the sugar. Add the egg, orange juice and vanilla and beat well.
3. Sift or mix together the salt, baking soda and flour. Stir into the batter. Add the rolled oats and chocolate chips.
4. Use about 1 tbsp/15 mL batter for each cookie and flatten. Bake for 10 to 12 minutes. Cool on racks.

ESPECIALLY FOR KIDS

Pretzel Cookies

Makes 5 dozen cookies

Kids seem to love things that look like something else. So these pretzel cookies usually are a big hit. Use coarse sugar to resemble the salt.

You can also use this dough for rolled cookies and cut them with cookie cutters. My children like shapes that don't come in cookie cutters, so often I cut free-form specialty shapes just for them. Picky, picky, picky!

	1 cup	unsalted butter	250 mL
	1½ cups	sugar	375 mL
	2	eggs	2
	1 tsp	pure vanilla extract	5 mL
	3 cups	all-purpose flour	750 mL
TOPPING	1	egg	1
	½ cup	coarse sugar or demerara sugar	125 mL

1 Preheat the oven to 375°F/190°C. Butter the cookie sheets with unsalted butter or line with parchment paper.

2 Beat the butter until light. Slowly beat in the sugar. Add the eggs one at a time and beat well. Add the vanilla.

3 Stir in the flour. If the dough is too soft to handle, refrigerate it until it can be rolled and shaped.

4 Use about 2 tbsp/25 mL dough for each cookie. Roll the dough into a long strip. Make a circle with ties overlapping and then twist once. Turn the twisted end over the circle to form a pretzel, as shown.

5 Arrange the pretzels on the cookie sheets. Beat the egg and brush on top of the cookies. Sprinkle with sugar. Bake for 12 to 15 minutes (or longer) until golden.

Note: *For rolled cookies, chill the dough until it is easy to roll. Cut into shapes, brush with the egg, sprinkle with sugar and bake for 8 to 10 minutes (the rolled cookies are thinner than the pretzels and will take less time to bake).*

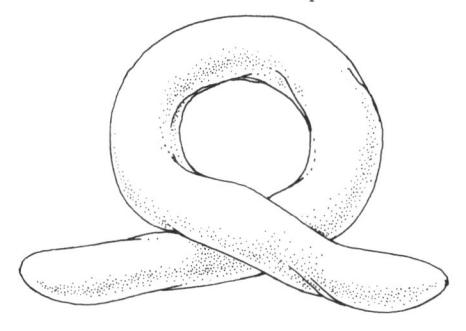

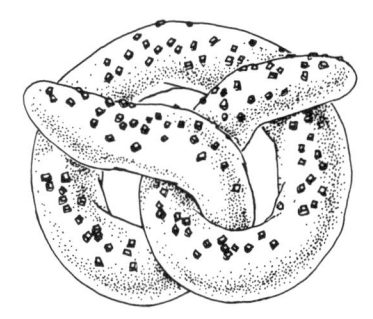

Chocolate Chip Cookies

Makes 4 dozen cookies

Chocolate chip cookies can be plain or fancy, but they are always popular. You can use chocolate chips or, for a more sophisticated version, chop up European bittersweet chocolate and use that instead. Chopped toasted pecans are also a fabulous addition, but they are optional—many children are allergic to or do not like nuts. (In fact, some children are also allergic to chocolate—use carob chips instead.) For a fun change, you can put Smarties in the cookies instead of chocolate chips.

1 cup	unsalted butter	250 mL
½ cup	brown sugar	125 mL
½ cup	granulated sugar	125 mL
1 tsp	pure vanilla extract	5 mL
1	egg	1
2 cups	all-purpose flour	500 mL
¼ tsp	salt	1 mL
1 tsp	baking soda	5 mL
1 cup	chocolate chips	250 mL
1 cup	chopped toasted pecans (optional)	250 mL

1. Butter the cookie sheets or line them with parchment paper.
2. Cream the butter with the sugars until light. Add the vanilla and egg and beat well.
3. Sift the flour with the salt and baking soda and add to the batter. Stir in the chocolate chips and nuts. Refrigerate the batter for 1 to 2 hours.
4. Preheat the oven to 375°F/190°C. Shape the cookies into balls about 1½ in/7 cm in diameter and arrange on cookie sheets. Press down slightly.
5. Bake for 8 to 10 minutes. The longer the cookies bake, the crisper they will be.

ESPECIALLY FOR KIDS

Stained-glass Cookies

Makes 4 dozen large cookies

These cookies are so adorable and delicious that they are worth the time and effort it takes to make them. They can be used as Christmas tree decorations, you can make a mobile with them, they are great for parties and party favours and children can even wear them as jewellery!

1 cup	unsalted butter	250 mL
1¼ cups	sugar	300 mL
¼ cup	water	50 mL
3 cups	all-purpose flour	750 mL
½ tsp	baking soda	2 mL
¼ tsp	salt	1 mL
5	25-g packages Lifesavers, different colours	5

1. Beat the butter until light and slowly add the sugar. Add the water and stir until smooth.
2. Sift or mix the flour with the baking soda and salt. Stir into the butter mixture. Knead it together well. (If the dough is very dry add a little more water.)
3. Wrap in plastic wrap and chill for 30 minutes.
4. Preheat the oven to 350°F/180°C. Line cookie sheets with parchment paper.
5. Roll pieces of dough into long ropes about ½-in/1-cm thick. Form the ropes into shapes, such as fish, boats, windows, houses, Christmas trees, etc. Press any pieces that touch each other together so that they do not separate while baking. Bake for 5 minutes.
6. Meanwhile, crush the Lifesavers, keeping each colour separate.
7. Fill in the holes between the ropes with different colours of candy. Bake for 5 to 6 minutes longer or until the candy melts. Cool.

ESPECIALLY FOR KIDS

Chocolate-coated Strawberries

Makes 15 large strawberries

Serve these chocolate-dipped strawberries as a dessert, snack, or as a garnish for chocolate mousse. Although they are very easy to prepare, there are a number of tricks that make them easier.

The berries should be dry when they are dipped into the chocolate. Some berries do not even need washing—wiping with a damp cloth is enough. If they are sandy and need washing, be sure to dry them thoroughly, because a little water in the chocolate could cause the chocolate to seize.

If the strawberry greens are nice, leave the greens on and use them as a handle for dipping. If they are not in good condition, hull the berries and dip the fatter end, grasping the point when dipping.

I like to use European bittersweet chocolate for the berries, but chocolate chips or domestic semisweet will also be fine. Coating chocolate (chocolate that contains more fat and therefore glazes well) can be used and the finished berries will look shinier, but I prefer the taste of the bittersweet chocolate.

15	large strawberries	15
12 oz	bittersweet chocolate	375 g

1 Clean and dry the strawberries.

2 Melt the chocolate gently over hot water or in the microwave. (When melting chocolate, always remove it from the heat before it is completely melted. Stir to complete the melting. That way there is no chance of burning it.)

3 Dip the strawberries halfway in the chocolate and set them on a waxed paper-lined cookie sheet. Allow them to set in the refrigerator for about 30 minutes.

ESPECIALLY FOR KIDS

Jelly Squares

Makes 36 squares

These colourful wiggly squares are a delight for all children. They love to make them, they love to play with them (ugh!) and they love to eat them. They make a great treat when it's your turn to bring snack at play group.

This recipe came from Patti Linzon's nanny, Tomasa. Patti's daughter, Mia, is one of Mark's favourite girlfriends. When we were testing these jelly squares, we used all kinds of flavour and colour combinations, and many children tested them. My editor Shelley Tanaka's children, Claire and Jessica, ate dozens of them. Anna loves them in any colour, but Mark of course is very selective and will only eat red, yellow and green squares!

3	**85-g packages Jello, in different colours**	3
3 cups	boiling water	750 mL
3½	envelopes unflavoured gelatine	3½
½ cup	milk	125 mL
2 tsp	sugar	10 mL

1 Empty one package Jello into a mixing bowl. Stir in 1 cup/250 mL boiling water. Stir to dissolve. Slowly mix in one envelope unflavoured gelatine, stirring constantly. Pour into the bottom of a 9-in x 13-in/3-L pan (for thin layers) or 8-in/20-cm baking pan (for thicker squares). Refrigerate until completely set, about 15 to 20 minutes.

2 Place the milk in small saucepan. Add the sugar. Sprinkle with half an envelope of unflavoured gelatine. Heat gently and stir to dissolve.

3 When the first layer is set, pour on half the milk mixture. Chill until set, about 10 minutes.

4 Repeat Step 1 with another colour of Jello and pour over the set milk layer. Refrigerate until set, about 15 to 20 minutes.

5 Pour the remaining milk mixture on top. Chill until set.

6 Repeat Step 1 with the remaining Jello and pour over the milk layer. Chill again until set.

7 Cut the jelly into squares or fancy shapes with large cookie cutters.

ESPECIALLY FOR KIDS

Maureen's Hamburger Cake

Makes one large cake

This cake is wonderful for both children and adults. It was first made for me by Maureen Lollar, who worked for me for many years. She has a wonderful sense of humour—as shown by this cake! Because some of the icing is butterscotch, and some is chocolate, the finished cake looks just like a hamburger, complete with strawberry jam "ketchup" and sesame seeds on top. (We gave George Cohon, President of McDonald's Canada, one of these cakes when CKFM participated in Ronald McDonald Day—he said he hoped we wouldn't go into competition with him!)

	3 oz	unsweetened chocolate	100 g
	1 cup	boiling water	250 mL
	1 tsp	baking soda	5 mL
	2¼ cups	cake and pastry flour	550 mL
	½ tsp	salt	2 mL
	2½ tsp	baking powder	12 mL
	½ cup	unsalted butter	125 mL
	2½ cups	granulated sugar	625 mL
	3	eggs, separated	3
	1 tsp	pure vanilla extract	5 mL
	1 cup	sour cream (preferably Astro)	250 mL
ICING	1¼ cups	unsalted butter	300 mL
	2 cups	brown sugar	500 mL
	½ cup	milk	125 mL
	4 cups	icing sugar, sifted	1 L
	2 tbsp	cocoa	25 mL
GARNISH	1 cup	strawberry jam or preserves	250 mL
	1 tbsp	toasted sesame seeds	15 mL

1 Preheat the oven to 350°F/180°C. Butter an 8- or 9-in/22- or 24-cm round cake pan and line the bottom with parchment paper or waxed paper. Butter an 8- or 9-in/22- or 24-cm 2 qt/2 L round-bottomed Pyrex casserole bowl and line the bottom with paper.

2 To make the cake, combine the chocolate and water in the top of a double boiler. Heat over gently simmering water until melted. Stir well and cool slightly. Add the baking soda.

3 Sift together the flour, salt and baking powder and reserve.

4 Cream the butter until light. Gradually beat in 2 cups/500 mL granulated sugar. Add the egg yolks, one at a time, and then add the vanilla.

5 Add the chocolate mixture to the egg yolk mixture. Add the dry ingredients alternately with the sour cream, mixing just until the ingredients are blended.

ESPECIALLY FOR KIDS

6 Beat the egg whites until light and gradually beat in the remaining ½ cup/125 mL granulated sugar. Fold the whites gently but thoroughly into the batter.

7 Pour the batter into the round cake pan until it is three-quarters full. Pour the remaining batter into the Pyrex casserole bowl. Bake for 40 to 50 minutes or until the cakes feel firm when gently pressed at the top. Let the cakes cool for 10 minutes and then remove from the pans. Cool on racks.

8 When cakes are cool, prepare the icing. Melt the butter in a saucepan. Add the brown sugar and cook for 2 minutes. Add the milk and bring to a boil. Cool.

9 Beat in the sifted icing sugar until the icing is of spreading consistency. If it is too runny, add more sugar; if it too stiff, add 1 tbsp/15 mL boiling water. Remove ½ cup/125 mL icing and mix with the cocoa.

10 To assemble, slice the cake from the round pan into two, horizontally. Place one half on a cake plate. Ice the top and sides with the butterscotch icing. Place the second half on top and ice with the cocoa frosting. Spoon on the jam, allowing it to flow down the sides of the cake like ketchup. Place the large, casserole-shaped cake on top with the rounded side up. Spread with butterscotch icing. Sprinkle the top with sesame seeds.

Peanut Butter Mousse Pie

Serves 8

When I was pregnant with Mark, I ate many peanut butter and jam sandwiches every day. People would come into the shop and would always ask what I was eating, expecting it to be something very exotic. I always felt they were terribly disappointed when I told them it was peanut butter and jam. And not even homemade.

At first I thought only children would like this pie. And me, of course. But I was wrong. Lots of people love peanut butter.

CRUST	1 cup	chocolate wafer cookie crumbs (approx. 20 wafers)	250 mL
	¼ cup	unsalted butter, melted	50 mL
FILLING	1 cup	peanut butter, smooth or crunchy	250 mL
	½ cup	unsalted butter	125 mL
	1 cup	sugar	250 mL
	2	egg yolks	2
	1 tsp	pure vanilla extract	5 mL
	1½ cups	whipping cream	375 mL
	2	Crispy Crunch chocolate bars (45 g each), chopped or ¾ cup/175 mL chocolate chips	2

1 To make the crust, combine the chocolate wafer crumbs and melted butter. Press into the bottom and sides of a 9-in/23-cm pie dish.

2 To make the filling, beat the peanut butter with ½ cup/125 mL butter until light and fluffy. Beat in the sugar. Add the egg yolks and vanilla and beat well.

3 Beat the cream until light and soft peaks form. Fold it into the peanut butter mixture with the chopped Crispy Crunch bars or chocolate chips.

4 Mound into the pie shell. Refrigerate for at least 2 hours before serving.

Easy Apple Crisp

Serves 8

Kids love to make apple crisp because it is so easy and tastes so great. This one is especially easy, so it is a good one to start children cooking with. You can teach them to use a vegetable peeler and they love removing the core neatly with a melon baller.

This is a great recipe to make the day after Halloween if your children have received a lot of apples. The kids don't mind not eating the apples if they can take part in their (the apples, that is) fate.

The first year Mark went trick-or-treating, he was quite terrified. After three houses, however, he started to get the hang of it. For days after, he kept knocking on doors (washrooms and cupboards included), expecting people to hand him goodies!

	8	apples (Spy or Golden Delicious work the best)	8
	1 tbsp	lemon juice	15 mL
TOPPING	1 cup	all-purpose flour	250 mL
	1 cup	brown sugar	250 mL
	1 tsp	cinnamon	5 mL
	¼ tsp	salt	1 mL
	½ cup	unsalted butter, cold, cut into bits	125 mL

1. Preheat the oven to 375°F/190°C. Butter a 9-in x 13-in/3-L baking dish.
2. Peel, halve and core the apples. Slice them thinly. Arrange in the baking dish and sprinkle with lemon juice.
3. Combine the flour with the sugar, cinnamon and salt. Add the butter and cut it in with a pastry blender or your fingertips.
4. Sprinkle the mixture over the apples and bake until the apples are very tender, 45 to 50 minutes. Serve with ice cream.

ESPECIALLY FOR KIDS

Grape Popsicles

Makes 8 popsicles (2 oz/60 mL each)

Whenever I used to make popsicles for my kids, the popsicles melted so quickly that more of it ended up on the front of their shirts than in their mouths. One of my assistants at the cooking school, Sue Roberts, solved my problem when she told me about some popsicles she used to make as a child. They had gelatine (Jello) in them and therefore did not melt nearly as quickly. She made them in many flavours, but grape was always her favourite because it was nice and tart.

Use your imagination or your child's taste preferences to combine flavours. Taste the mixture before freezing and add a little sugar if you think you need it.

(Many listeners have written to say they are relieved to know that I will occasionally use prepackaged commercial ingredients, like Jello.)

1	85-g package grape Jello	1
1 cup	boiling water	250 mL
1 cup	cold water	250 mL
1	6-g package unsweetened grape Kool-Aid	1

1. Combine the Jello with the boiling water until dissolved.
2. Stir in the cold water and Kool-Aid. Pour the mixture into popsicle moulds (or ice cube trays) and insert sticks. Freeze until firm.

ESPECIALLY FOR KIDS

Monster Slush

Serves 4

This drink is perfect to serve on Halloween. It is orange and the straw (licorice) is black. If the slush is too thick to be slurped up through the licorice, stir the drinks until they melt more.

The idea for this recipe came from Jane Somerville, the publisher of this book. Her kids, Julian and Jordan, love this drink! I love it, too. It reminds me of Creamsicles.

¾ cup	frozen orange juice concentrate	175 mL
1 pint	vanilla ice cream	500 mL
4	black licorice twisters	4

1. Place the orange juice and ice cream in a blender or food processor. Blend together until very smooth. Pour the drink into glasses. (It is usually quite thick. If you want it thinner, process more or stir to melt.)
2. Cut the ends off licorice twisters and cut to fit the glasses as straws.

Gwen's Tomato Macaroni and Cheese

Serves 4

Tomato soup lovers often say that nothing beats Campbell's tomato soup. I don't know whether this is because of their childhood memories, or whether the soup is really terrific, because as a child I would never eat anything red. In fact, I'm still not a tomato soup fan, but I do love this macaroni and cheese.

Nothing could be faster and easier than this. And it is great for kids of all ages. My friend, Gwen Fargeon, is one of the best cooks I know, so when she told me about this recipe, I knew it would be good. And it is.

8 oz	macaroni	250 g
1	10-oz/284-g tin Campbell's plain tomato soup, undiluted	1
½ tsp	salt	2 mL
1½ cups	grated Cheddar cheese	375 mL
¼ cup	unsalted butter, cut into bits	50 mL

1 Cook the macaroni in a large pot of boiling, salted water until tender, 8 to 10 minutes. Drain well and shake out the water. Do not rinse.

2 Preheat the oven to 400°F/200°C. Butter a 8-in/1.5-L square baking dish.

3 Combine the macaroni with the undiluted soup, salt and cheese. Mix well. Pour into the prepared dish. Dot with butter.

4 Bake for 50 to 60 minutes until the top is browned and bubbly.

ESPECIALLY
FOR KIDS

Playdough

If you like to make things with your children, you will have noticed that playdough recipes are everywhere. This particular one was brought to my attention at Mark's playgroup, organized by Launnie Garetson and Jennifer Werry. Lynn Saunders, my role model and mother of four beautiful girls, Lyndsey, Natasha, Bethany and Megan, perfected the recipe for me. It's softer and smoother than any playdough I have ever bought (and it doesn't smell funny!).

As well as rolling it into fancy shapes, I like to make miniature vegetables with Mark and Anna, and we have pretend sophisticated dinner parties.

Homemade playdough makes nice Christmas presents and fantastic party favours—include one or two plastic cookie cutters with it. Store it in a tightly sealed plastic container, and it will last for a long time.

1 cup	all-purpose flour	250 mL
½ cup	salt	125 mL
2 tbsp	cream of tartar	25 mL
1 cup	water	250 mL
2 tbsp	vegetable oil	25 mL
	Food colouring*	

1 Combine the flour, salt and cream of tartar in a saucepan and stir together to blend.

2 Combine the water and oil.

3 Stir the liquid into the flour mixture until smooth. Cook over medium heat until the mixture forms a ball, about 5 minutes.

4 Turn out onto the counter and knead until smooth. Divide into two or three sections and colour each section with a different colour (use lots of colour). Store in a sealed container.

* *Use the paste food colourings if you can find them. The colours will be more intense and vibrant.*

Index

A Almond
    Amaretto trifle, 148
    apricot almond quickbread, 115
    cajun spiced almonds, 18
    fruitcake with Amaretto, 130
Amaretto
    fruitcake, 130
    trifle, 148
Anna Banana's birthday cake, 132
Appetizers, 10-25 (*see also* Light meals; Pastas; Soups)
    almonds, cajun spiced, 18
    Bugialli's fresh tomato sauce with spaghetti, 78
    chèvre spread, 17
    chicken wings, Szechuan orange, 23
    crêpes with smoked salmon and cream cheese, 14
    fettuccine California style, 80
    fettuccine with ham and asparagus, 74
    fettuccine with smoked chicken and hazelnuts, 71
    linguine with smoked salmon and lemon sauce, 72
    olivada and Mascarpone torta, 20
    olive mustard spread, 11
    oriental pesto with noodles, 73
    penne with creamy sausage sauce, 76
    penne with mixed sausages and red peppers, 70
    salad, grilled Carpaccio, 19
    salad, Muffalata olive, 15
    scallops Provençal, 22
    shrimp balls, hundred corner, 16
    smoked salmon canapés, 12
    smoked salmon pâté, 13
    smoked trout tartare, 21
    spaghetti alla Carbonara, 77
    spaghetti with pesto sauce, 82
    spaghetti with seafood sauce, 75
    spaghettini with sun-dried tomatoes, 81
    vegetables with rouille, 24-25

Apple
    apple oatmeal bread, 116
    apple, pear and apricot pie, 158
    apple pie cake, 131
    caramelized apple pancakes, 84
    easy apple crisp, 179
Applesauce, caramelized, 156
Apricot
    apple, pear and apricot pie, 158
    apricot almond quickbread, 115
    apricot-glazed chicken, 56
Artichokes
    Muffalata olive salad, 15
Asparagus
    asparagus Marco Polo, 89
    fettuccine with ham and asparagus, 74
    scallop and asparagus soup, 28

B Balsamic vinegar dressing, 100
Banana
    banana cake, 132
    mini banana muffins, 169
Barbecued dishes
    barbecued brisket, 53
    barbecued potatoes and onions, 96
    Chinese barbecued ribs, 67
    deviled chicken, 55
    grilled Carpaccio salad, 19
    lemon mint lamb chops, 62
    marinated flank steak, 48
    marmalade-glazed leg of lamb, 61
    mustard-glazed sirloin steak, 52
    spicy burger, 54
    Western barbecued pork chops, 65
    whisky-glazed steak, 47
Barley
    beef and barley soup with wild mushrooms, 36
Basil
    cold cream of tomato soup with basil, 34
    tomatoes with basil parmesan dressing, 101

Beans
    green bean soup with lemon chive butter, 40
    pasta e fagioli, 39
Beef
    barbecued brisket, 53
    beef and barley soup with wild mushrooms, 36
    grilled Carpaccio salad, 19
    spicy burgers, 54
    steak, blackened sirloin, 51
    steak, marinated flank, 48
    steak, mustard-glazed, 52
    steak salad with mustard dressing, 105
    steak, whisky-glazed, 47
    steak with green peppercorn sauce, 50
    steak with mustard cream sauce, 49
Belgian endive
    in salad, 103
    soup, 29
Black beans
    steamed salmon and ginger with black bean sauce, 43
Blackened sirloin steak, 51
Blueberry
    banana blueberry muffins, 117
    blueberry lemon mousse pie, 160-161
Breads, 113-116
    apple oatmeal, 116
    apricot almond, 115
    banana blueberry muffins, 117
    bread pudding, 155
    brioche, 118-119
    cornbread muffins, 123
    cornbread stuffing, 58
    cornbread with cheese custard filling, 113
    fresh date and yogurt muffins, 122
    Labour of Love sticky buns, 120-121
    mini banana muffins, 169
    orange pecan muffins, 124
    whole wheat, 114
Brioche, 118-119
Brisket, barbecued, 53

INDEX

Broccoli
   stir-fried scallops with broccoli, 44
Brownies, soufflé, 138
Bugialli's fresh tomato sauce with spaghetti, 78
Bulgur wheat pilaf, 95
Buns, sticky, 120-121
Burgers, spicy, 54
Butter
   green bean soup with lemon chive butter, 40
   butter tarts, 163
Butterscotch icing, 176-177

C Cajun dishes
   blackened sirloin steak, 51
   Gumbo Ya Ya, 35
   spiced almonds, 18
   voodoo chicken with cornbread stuffing, 58-59
Cakes, 125-135 (*see also* Desserts)
   Amaretto trifle, 148
   Anna Banana's birthday cake, 132
   fruitcake with Amaretto, 130
   Maureen's hamburger cake, 176-177
   mini carrot cakes with cream cheese icing, 134-135
   Mocha trifle, 126-127
   mud cake with fudge glaze, 133
   peach upside-down cake, 129
   Ray's square apple pie cake, 131
   soufflé brownies, 138
   sponge cake, 128
   wacky cake, 168
California style fettuccine, 80
Canapés, smoked salmon, 12
Candied sweet potatoes, 94
Capers
   sole with lemon and capers, 45
Caramel
   caramel corn, 166
   caramelized apple pancakes, 84
   caramelized applesauce, 156
   coffee crème caramel, 150
   coffee ice cream with caramel sauce, 154

Carrot
   carrot flowers, 25
   mini carrot cakes with cream cheese icing, 134-135
Cheese
   cheese-baked vegetable custard, 92
   cheese tart with yeast pastry, 83
   chèvre spread, 17
   corn soup with herb cheese, 31
   cornbread with cheese custard filling, 113
   crêpes with smoked salmon and cream cheese, 14
   fettuccine California style, 80
   macaroni and cheese, 79
   olivada and Mascarpone torta, 20
   rugalahs, 141
   tomato macaroni and cheese, 182
   tomatoes with basil parmesan dressing, 101
Chèvre
   fettuccine California style, 80
   spread, 17
Chicken, 55-60·
   apricot-glazed chicken, 56
   chicken soup, 27
   chicken with raspberry vinegar, 57
   Chinese emerald chicken, 60
   deviled chicken, 55
   fettuccine with smoked chicken and hazelnuts, 71
   Szechuan orange chicken wings, 23
   voodoo chicken with cornbread stuffing, 58-59
Children's recipes, 165-183
Chinese dishes
   Chinese barbecued ribs, 67
   Chinese emerald chicken, 60
   Chinese-style pork, 68
   hundred corner shrimp balls, 16
   steamed salmon and ginger with black bean sauce, 43
   stir-fried scallops with broccoli, 44
   sweet and sour spareribs, 66
   Szechuan orange chicken wings, 23

Chives
   potato salad with olives and chopped chives, 102
Chocolate
   chocolate blizzard cookies, 140
   chocolate chip cookies, 172
   chocolate chip oatmeal cookies, 170
   chocolate-coated strawberries, 174
   chocolate mousse, 149, 167
   chocolate squares, 138
   chocolate truffles with Grand Marnier, 142
   hazelnut chocolates, 144
   hot chocolate sauce, 152
   mud cake with fudge glaze, 133
   raspberry truffles, 143
   wacky cake, 168
Chops
   lemon mint lamb chops, 62
   Western barbecued pork chops, 65
Chowder, seafood, 33
Cinnamon crescents, 141
Clams
   seafood chowder, 33
Coffee
   coffee crème caramel, 150
   coffee ice cream with caramel sauce, 154
   mocha trifle cake, 126-127
Cold spaghetti salad, 107
Cookies, 137-141, 170-173
   chocolate blizzard cookies, 140
   chocolate chip cookies, 172
   chocolate chip oatmeal cookies, 170
   pretzel cookies, 171
   rugalahs, 141
   Sarah Band's lemon squares, 139
   shortbread, 137
   soufflé brownies, 138
   stained-glass cookies, 173
Corn
   caramel corn, 166
   corn soup with herb cheese, 31

INDEX

Cornbread
  cornbread muffins, 123
  cornbread stuffing, 58-59
  cornbread with cheese custard filling, 113
Cream cheese
  crêpes, 14
  icing, 134-135
Crêpes with smoked salmon and cream cheese, 14
Crescents, cinnamon, 141
Crisp
  easy apple crisp, 179
  rhubarb crisp, 161
Curried pureed parsnips, 93

D Date and yogurt muffins, 122
Deep-dish fruit pie, 158
Desserts, 145-157 (*see also* Cakes; Cookies; Puddings)
  Amaretto trifle, 148
  apple crisp, 179
  apple, pear and apricot pie, 158
  apple pie cake, 131
  blueberry lemon mousse pie, 160-161
  bread pudding, 155
  butter tarts, 163
  caramel corn, 166
  caramelized applesauce, 156
  chocolate-coated strawberries, 174
  chocolate mousse, 149, 167
  coffee crème caramel, 150
  coffee ice cream with caramel sauce, 154
  fresh fruit tarts, 162
  fresh peach pie, 159
  frozen Grand Marnier soufflé with hot chocolate sauce, 152
  grape popsicles, 180
  jelly squares, 175
  maple syrup mousse, 147
  Maureen's hamburger cake, 176-177
  mocha trifle cake, 126-127
  peach flambé, 157
  peach upside-down cake, 129
  peanut butter mousse pie, 178
  raspberry yogurt mousse, 153
  rhubarb crisp, 161
  rice pudding, 151
  Russian mousse with strawberry sauce, 146
  soufflé brownies, 138

Deviled chicken, 55
Dill
  spinach soup with dill and lemon, 32
Dim Sum
  hundred corner shrimp balls, 16
Dips (*see also* Spreads)
  vegetables with rouille, 24-25
Dressings (salad), 100-111
  Balsamic vinegar, 100
  basil parmesan, 101
  creamy, 103
  homemade mayonnaise, 111
  mustard, 105
  Niçoise, 104
  tarragon, 110
  vinaigrette, 109
Drinks
  monster slush, 181

E Endives
  Belgian endive salad, 103
  Belgian endive soup, 29

F Fennel
  fennel and black olive salad, 108
  fennel and leek soup, 30
Fettuccine
  California style, 80
  with ham and asparagus, 74
  with smoked chicken and hazelnuts, 71
Fish and seafood
  crêpes with smoked salmon and cream cheese, 14
  grilled tiger shrimp, 42
  lemon salmon Teriyaki, 46
  linguine with smoked salmon and lemon sauce, 72
  salmon appetizers, 12-14
  scallops Provençal, 22
  smoked trout tartare, 21
  sole with lemon and capers, 45
  spaghetti with seafood sauce, 75
  steamed salmon and ginger with black bean sauce, 43
  stir-fried scallops with broccoli, 44
Flambé, peach, 157

Frozen Grand Marnier soufflé, 152
Fruit
  apple crisp, 179
  apple oatmeal bread, 116
  apple pancakes, 84
  apple, pear and apricot pie, 158
  apple pie cake, 131
  apricot almond quickbread, 115
  banana blueberry muffins, 117
  banana cake, 132
  blueberry lemon mousse pie, 160-161
  caramelized applesauce, 156
  chocolate-coated strawberries, 174
  date and yogurt muffins, 122
  fruit tarts, 162
  fruitcake with Amaretto, 130
  mini banana muffins, 169
  orange pecan muffins, 124
  peach flambé, 157
  peach pie, 159
  peach upside-down cake, 129
  raspberry yogurt mousse, 153
  rhubarb crisp, 161
  strawberry sauce, 146
Fruitcake with Amaretto, 130
Fudge
  mud cake with fudge glaze, 133

G Garlic
  vegetables with rouille, 24-25
Goat cheese
  chèvre spread, 17
  fettuccine California-style, 80
Grand Marnier
  chocolate truffles with Grand Marnier, 142
  Grand Marnier soufflé with hot chocolate sauce, 152
Grape popsicles, 180
Green bean soup with lemon chive butter, 40
Green peppercorn sauce, 50
Grilled dishes
  grilled Carpaccio salad, 19
  grilled tiger shrimp, 42
  marinated flank steak, 48
  mustard-glazed sirloin steak, 52
  whisky-glazed steak, 47

INDEX

Gumbo Ya Ya, 35
Gwen's tomato macaroni and cheese, 182

H Ham
    fettuccine with ham and asparagus, 74
    split pea soup with smoked ham, 38
Hamburger cake, 176-177
Hamburgers, spicy, 54
Hazelnuts
    fettuccine with smoked chicken and hazelnuts, 71
    hazelnut chocolates, 144
Homemade mayonnaise, 111
Hors d'oeuvres *see* Appetizers
Hundred corner shrimp balls, 16

I Icing
    butterscotch, 176-177
    cream cheese, 134-135
    fudge glaze, 133
Ice cream
    coffee ice cream with caramel sauce, 154
    frozen Grand Marnier soufflé, 152

J Japanese dishes
    glazed zucchini with sesame, 88
    lemon salmon Teriyaki, 46
Jelly squares, 175

K Kids' recipes, 165-183

L Labour of Love sticky buns, 120-121
Lamb
    lemon mint lamb chops, 62
    marmalade-glazed leg of lamb, 61
Latkes, potato, 98
Leek
    fennel and leek soup, 30

Lemon
    blueberry lemon mousse pie, 160-161
    lemon chive butter, 40
    lemon mint lamb chops, 62
    lemon salmon Teriyaki, 46
    lemon sole with capers, 45
    lemon squares, 139
    linguine with smoked salmon and lemon sauce, 72
    spinach soup with dill and lemon, 32
Lettuce, types of, 103
Light meals (*see also* Pastas)
    beef and barley soup with wild mushrooms, 36
    caramelized apple pancakes, 84
    cheese tart with yeast pastry, 83
    Gumbo Ya Ya, 35
    macaroni and cheese, 79, 182
    Passover bubelechs, 85
    potato latkes, 98
    salad Niçoise, 104
    seafood chowder, 33
    smoked chicken salad, 106
    split pea soup with smoked ham, 38
    steak salad with mustard dressing, 105
    tomato macaroni and cheese, 182
    yogurt pancakes, 165
Linguine with smoked salmon and lemon sauce, 72
Liver
    Provimi veal, 63

M Macaroni and cheese, 79
    for kids, 182
Main courses, 41-68
    barbecued brisket, 53
    cheese tart with yeast pastry, 83
    chicken, apricot-glazed, 56
    chicken, Chinese emerald, 60
    chicken, deviled, 55
    chicken salad, 106
    chicken, voodoo, with corn-bread stuffing, 58-59
    chicken wings, Szechuan orange, 23
    Chicken with raspberry vinegar, 57
    Chinese barbecued ribs, 67

    Chinese-style pork, 68
    fettuccine with ham and asparagus, 74
    fettuccine with smoked chicken and hazelnuts, 71
    grilled tiger shrimps, 42
    leg of lamb, marmalade-glazed, 61
    lemon mint lamb chops, 62
    lemon salmon Teriyaki, 46
    penne with creamy sausage sauce, 75
    penne with mixed sausages and red peppers, 70
    pork chops, Western barbecued, 65
    Provimi veal liver, 63
    salad Niçoise, 104
    sole with lemon and capers, 45
    spaghetti with seafood sauce, 75
    spicy burgers, 54
    steak, blackened sirloin, 51
    steak, marinated flank, 48
    steak, mustard-glazed, 52
    steak salad with mustard dressing, 105
    steak, whisky-glazed, 47
    steaks with green peppercorn sauce, 50
    steak with mustard cream sauce, 49
    steamed salmon and ginger with black bean sauce, 43
    stir-fried scallops with broccoli, 44
    sweet and sour spareribs, 66
    tomato macaroni and cheese, 182
    veal scaloppine with Marsala cream sauce, 64
Maple syrup mousse, 147
Marinated flank steak, 48
Marinated vegetable salad, 100
Marmalade-glazed leg of lamb, 61
Marsala cream sauce, 64
Mascarpone torta, 20
Mashed potatoes with wild mushrooms, 97
Matzah meal Passover bubelechs, 85
Maureen's hamburger cake, 176-177
Mayonnaise, homemade, 111
Mini banana muffins, 169
Mini carrot cakes, 134-135

INDEX

Mint
 lemon mint lamb chops, 62
Mixed peppers, 91
Mocha trifle cake, 126-127
Monster slush, 181
Mousse, savoury
 smoked salmon pâté, 13
Mousse, sweet
 blueberry lemon mousse pie, 160-161
 chocolate mousse, 149, 167
 maple syrup mousse, 147
 raspberry yogurt mousse, 153
 Russian mousse with strawberry sauce, 146
Muffins
 banana blueberry, 117
 cornbread, 123
 date and yogurt, 122
 mini banana, 169
 orange pecan, 124
Mushrooms
 beef and barley soup with wild mushrooms, 36
 mashed potatoes with wild mushrooms, 97
Mustard
 mustard dressing, 105
 mustard-glazed sirloin steak, 52
 olive mustard spread, 11
 steak with mustard cream sauce, 49

N New Wave salad, 103
Noodles *see* Pastas
Nuts
 cajun spiced almonds, 18
 fettuccine with smoked chicken and hazelnuts, 71
 oriental pesto with noodles, 73
 peanut butter mousse pie, 178
 spinach with raisins and pine nuts, 90

O Oatmeal
 apple oatmeal bread, 116
 chocolate chip oatmeal cookies, 170

Olives
 fennel and black olive salad, 108
 Muffalata olive salad, 15
 olivada and Mascarpone torta, 20
 olive mustard spread, 11
 potato salad with olives and chopped chives, 102
Onions
 barbecued potatoes and onions, 96
Orange
 orange drink, 181
 orange pecan muffins, 124
 Szechuan orange chicken wings, 23
Oriental pesto with noodles, 73

P Pancakes
 caramelized apple, 84
 Passover bubelechs, 85
 potato latkes, 98
 yogurt, 165
Parsley, types of, 73
Parsnips, curried pureed, 93
Passover recipes
 Passover bubelechs, 85
 soufflé brownies, 138
Pastas, 69-82 (*see also* Appetizers; Light meals)
 Bugialli's fresh tomato sauce with spaghetti, 78
 fettuccine California style, 80
 fettuccine with ham and asparagus, 74
 fettuccine with smoked chicken and hazelnuts, 71
 linguine with smoked salmon and lemon sauce, 72
 macaroni and cheese, 79, 182
 oriental pesto with noodles, 73
 pasta e fagioli, 39
 penne with creamy sausage sauce, 76
 penne with mixed sausages and red peppers, 70
 spaghetti alla Carbonara, 77
 spaghetti salad, 107
 spaghetti with pesto sauce, 82
 spaghetti with seafood sauce, 75
 spaghettini with sun-dried tomatoes, 81
 tomato macaroni and cheese, 182

Pastries *see* Pies
Pastry, yeast, 83
Pâté, smoked salmon, 13
Peach
 fresh peach pie, 159
 peach flambé, 157
 peach upside-down cake, 129
Peanut butter mousse pie, 178
Peanuts
 oriental pesto with noodles, 73
Pear
 apple, pear and apricot pie, 158
Peas
 split pea soup with smoked ham, 38
Pecan
 orange pecan muffins, 124
Penne
 with creamy sausage sauce, 76
 with mixed sausages and red peppers, 70
Peppers
 mixed, 91
 penne with mixed sausages and red peppers, 70
 sweet red pepper soup, 37
Pesto
 oriental pesto with noodles, 73
 spaghetti with pesto sauce, 82
Pies
 apple, pear and apricot pie, 158
 apple pie cake, 131
 blueberry lemon mousse pie, 160-161
 butter tarts, 163
 fruit tarts, 162
 peach pie, 159
 peanut butter mousse pie, 178
Pilaf, bulgur wheat, 95
Pine nuts
 spinach with raisins and pine nuts, 90
Playdough, 183
Popcorn, 166
Popsicles, grape, 180
Pork
 Chinese barbecued ribs, 67
 Chinese-style pork, 68
 sweet and sour spareribs, 66
 Western barbecued pork chops, 65

INDEX

Potatoes
    candied sweet potatoes, 94
    mashed potatoes with wild mushrooms, 97
    salad Niçoise, 104
    potato latkes, 98
    potato salad with olives and chopped chives, 102
    smoked chicken salad, 106
Pretzel cookies, 171
Provençal, scallops, 22
Provimi veal liver, 63
Pudding
    bread pudding, 155
    rice pudding, 151

Q Quickbreads
    apricot almond, 115
    banana blueberry muffins, 117
    cornbread muffins, 123
    cornbread with cheese custard filling, 113
    date and yogurt muffins, 122
    mini banana muffins, 169
    orange pecan muffins, 124

R Raspberry
    chicken with raspberry vinegar, 57
    raspberry truffles, 143
    raspberry yogurt mousse, 153
Ray's square apple pie cake, 131
Red pepper
    mixed peppers, 91
    sweet red pepper soup, 37
Rhubarb crisp, 161
Ribs, Chinese barbecued, 67
Rice pudding, 151
Rolls (*see also* Breads; Quickbreads)
    sticky buns, 120-121
Rouille, 24-25
Rugalahs, 141
Russian mousse, 146

S Salad dressings, 100-111
    Balsamic vinegar, 100
    basil parmesan, 101
    creamy, 103
    homemade mayonnaise, 111
    mustard, 105
    Niçoise, 104
    tarragon, 110
    vinaigrette, 109

Salads, 100-108
    chicken, 106
    cold spaghetti, 107
    fennel and black olive, 108
    grilled Carpaccio, 19
    marinated vegetable salad, 100
    Muffalata olive salad, 15
    New Wave, 103
    Niçoise, 104
    potato salad with olives and chopped chives, 102
    steak salad with mustard dressing, 105
    tomatoes with basil parmesan dressing, 101
Salmon
    crêpes with smoked salmon and cream cheese, 14
    lemon salmon Teriyaki, 46
    linguine with smoked salmon and lemon sauce, 72
    smoked salmon canapés, 12
    smoked salmon pâté, 13
    steamed salmon and ginger with black bean sauce, 43
Sarah Band's lemon squares, 139
Sauces
    apple, 156
    caramel, 154
    green peppercorn, 50
    hot chocolate, 152
    lemon, 72
    marsala cream, 64
    mustard cream, 49
    strawberry, 146
Sausage
    Gumbo Ya Ya, 35
    penne with creamy sausage sauce, 76
    penne with mixed sausages and red peppers, 70
Scallops
    scallop and asparagus soup, 28
    scallops Provençal, 22
    seafood chowder, 33
    spaghetti with seafood sauce, 75
    stir-fried scallops with broccoli, 44
    veal scaloppine with marsala cream sauce, 64
Seafood *see* Fish and seafood
Sesame
    glazed zucchini with sesame, 88

Shortbread, 137
Shrimp
    grilled tiger shrimp, 42
    hundred corner shrimp balls, 16
    seafood chowder, 33
    spaghetti with seafood sauce, 75
Sirloin steak, mustard-glazed, 52
    (*see also* Steak)
Smoked chicken
    fettuccine with smoked chicken and hazelnuts, 71
    smoked chicken salad, 106
Smoked salmon
    crêpes with smoked salmon and cream cheese, 14
    smoked salmon canapés, 12
    smoked salmon pâté, 13
    smoked salmon with linguine and lemon sauce, 72
Smoked trout tartare, 21
Sole with lemon and capers, 45
Soufflé brownies, 138
Soufflé, frozen Grand Marnier, 152
Soups, 26-40
    beef and barley, with wild mushrooms, 36
    Belgian endive, 29
    chicken, 27
    cold cream of tomato with basil, 34
    corn, with herb cheese, 31
    fennel and leek, 30
    green bean, with lemon chive butter, 40
    Gumbo Ya Ya, 35
    pasta e fagioli, 39
    scallop and asparagus, 28
    seafood chowder, 33
    spinach, with dill and lemon, 32
    split pea, with smoked ham, 38
    sweet red pepper, 37
Spaghetti
    Bugialli's fresh tomato sauce with spaghetti, 78
    cold spaghetti salad, 107
    spaghetti alla Carbonara, 77
    spaghetti with pesto sauce, 82
    spaghetti with seafood sauce, 75
    spaghettini with sun-dried tomatoes, 81

INDEX

Spareribs, sweet and sour, 66
Spicy burgers, 54
Spinach
  spinach soup with dill and lemon, 32
  spinach with raisins and pine nuts, 90
Split pea soup with smoked ham, 38
Sponge cake, 128
Spreads
  chèvre, 17
  muffalata olive salad, 15
  olivada and Mascarpone torta, 20
  olive mustard, 11
  smoked salmon canapés, 12
  smoked trout tartare, 21
Squares
  jelly squares, 175
  lemon squares, 139
  soufflé brownies, 138
Stained-glass cookies, 173
Steak
  blackened sirloin, 51
  marinated flank, 48
  mustard-glazed, 52
  steak salad with mustard dressing, 105
  whisky-glazed, 47
  with green peppercorn sauce, 50
  with mustard cream sauce, 49
Steamed salmon and ginger with black bean sauce, 43
Sticky buns, 120-121
Stir-fried dishes
  Chinese emerald chicken, 60
  stir-fried scallops with broccoli, 44
Stock, chicken, 27
Strawberries
  chocolate-coated strawberries, 174
  Russian mousse with strawberry sauce, 146
Stuffing, cornbread, 58-59
Sweet potatoes, candied, 94
Sweet red pepper soup, 37
Sweet and sour spareribs, 66
Swiss chard Italian style, 87
Szechuan orange chicken wings, 23

T Tarragon salad dressing, 110
Tarts
  butter tarts, 163
  cheese tart with yeast pastry, 83
  fresh fruit tarts, 162
  peanut butter mousse pie, 178
Teriyaki, lemon salmon, 46
Tiger shrimps, grilled, 42
Tomatoes
  Bugialli's fresh tomato sauce with spaghetti, 78
  cold cream of tomato soup with basil, 34
  sun-dried tomatoes with spaghettini, 81
  tomato macaroni and cheese, 182
  tomatoes with basil parmesan dressing, 101
Trifle
  Amaretto, 148
  mocha trifle cake, 126-127
Trout
  smoked trout tartare, 21
Truffles
  chocolate truffles with Grand Marnier, 142
  hazelnut chocolate truffles, 144
  raspberry truffles, 143

U Upside-down cake, peach, 129

V Veal
  Provimi veal liver, 63
  veal scaloppine with marsala cream sauce, 64
Vegetables
  asparagus Marco Polo, 89
  barbecued potatoes and onions, 96
  bulgur wheat pilaf, 95
  candied sweet potatoes, 94
  cheese-baked vegetable custard, 92
  curried pureed parsnips, 93
  glazed zucchini with sesame, 88
  marinated vegetable salad, 100
  mashed potatoes with wild mushrooms, 97
  mixed peppers, 91
  potato latkes, 98
  spinach with raisins and pine nuts, 90
  Swiss chard Italian style, 87
  vegetables with rouille, 24-25
Vinaigrette, 109
Vinegar
  chicken with raspberry vinegar, 57
Voodoo chicken with cornbread stuffing, 58-59

W Wacky cake, 168
Western barbecued pork chops, 65
Whisky-glazed steak, 47
Whole wheat bread, 114

Y Yeast recipes
  apple oatmeal bread, 116
  brioche, 118-119
  cheese tart with yeast pastry, 83
  sticky buns, 120-121
  whole wheat bread, 114
Yogurt
  raspberry yogurt mousse, 153
  yogurt pancakes, 165

Z Zucchini, glazed, with sesame, 88

About Bonnie Stern

Bonnie Stern graduated from the University of Toronto in 1969 before taking the professional food administration and chef training program at George Brown College. After completing a two-year diploma course, training in restaurants, teaching cooking and learning the housewares business, she opened her own school and cookware shop in 1973. During this time she has studied with some of the best-known food specialists in the world—Simone (Simca) Beck in the south of France; at La Varenne in Paris; with Marcella Hazan in Italy; learning French Provincial cooking with Jacques Pépin; with Julie Dannenbaum; with Nina Simonds at the Wei-Chuan cooking school in Taipei; with Giuliano Bugialli; with Madeleine Kamman and many other exciting teachers. Bonnie is the author of three other cookbooks—*Food Processor Cuisine/La Cuisine Tourbillon, At My Table* and *Bonnie Stern's Cuisinart Cookbook.* In addition to her popular weekly radio spot with Judy Webb on CKFM's "Hour Toronto Magazine" for the past eight years, she freelances for Toronto's *Globe and Mail,* is a regular contributor to *Canadian Living* magazine, appears regularly on CTV's "Canada AM" and is a regular guest on CBC "Morningside" with Peter Gzowski.

Her school was the first Canadian cooking school to be written up by *Bon Appetit* magazine, and her recipes have appeared on both the 1985 and 1986 Milk Calendars.

Bonnie is a certified member of the International Association of Cooking Professionals and she was chairman of their sixth annual convention held in Toronto in 1984. Bonnie is also a professional member of the American Institute of Wine and Food and the Toronto Culinary Guild.

A Note on Metric

All the recipes in this book are given in both imperial and metric measurements. Follow a recipe in either imperial or metric, but do not try to use both and do not try to convert recipes yourself. Comparing the imperial and metric parts of a recipe can be confusing because the conversions are not always consistent or exact. In this book, 1 cup is replaced by 250 mL and each recipe is adjusted accordingly. So don't worry if the conversions do not follow a conversion table exactly. In some recipes, for example, ¼ cup is replaced by 50 mL and in some recipes 3 tbsp is replaced by 50 mL. But both will work because of the balance of the conversions of the other ingredients.

If you wish to follow the recipes in metric, buy a set of metric measures. They are worth the investment.